inv 277462
28/11/83

£39.20

H. Margret Berry

D1809284

Outstanding Dissertations in **Linguistics**

edited by
Jorge Hankamer ■ Harvard University

A Garland Series

Aspects of
the Grammar of Focus
in English

Adrian Akmajian

Garland Publishing, Inc.   ■   New York & London
1979

Library of Congress Cataloging in Publication Data

Akmajian, Adrian.
    Aspects of the grammar of focus in English.

    (Outstanding dissertations in linguistics)
    Originally presented as the author's thesis,
Massachusetts Institute of Technology, 1970.
    Bibliography: p.
    Includes index.
    1. English language—Grammar, Generative. I. Title.
II. Series.
PE1106.A4   1979   425   78-66534
ISBN 0-8240-9691-6

© 1979 Adrian Akmajian
All rights reserved

All volumes in this series are printed on acid-free,
250-year-life paper.
Printed in the United States of America

Preface

In the late 60's, certain linguists, notably Chomsky (1968) and Jackendoff (1969) were working on modifications of the so-called Standard Theory, largely concentrating on the contribution of surface structure to semantic interpretation of sentences. This line of research was often referred to as the "Interpretive Theory", and somewhat later as the "Lexicalist/Interpretive Theory", and one of the central concerns in this school of thought was showing that semantic features of a sentence such as logical scope relations involved in negation, quantification, and adverbs were determined by the surface structure representation of a sentence. This doctoral dissertation was an attempt to work out another area within the so-called "Interpretive" approach, namely focus-presupposition relations. Like other research in the general Interpretivist line, this dissertation sought to show that certain aspects of meaning could not be reasonably represented at the deep structure level, and proposed that an alternative system of representation had to be devised for focus-presupposition relations (summarized in Akmajian (1973)).

In the eight years since this thesis was written, we have seen a general abandonment of both the Standard Theory and its extreme variation, Generative Semantics. Linguists such as Chomsky and Lasnik (1977) and Bresnan (1978) have proposed theories in which "Deep Structure" is non-existent, and syntactic representations are all surface or near-surface structures. Further, transformational syntax has begun to merge with certain areas of artificial intelligence, cognitive psychology and philosophy, producing, once again, an exciting new line of research. The Interpretivist approach, then, to the extent that it was based on correct intuitions, not only led to a significant modification of classical TG, but also gradually led researchers into productive lines of new research.

In the area of focus specifically, the central ideas of Chapters 3 & 4 of this thesis appeared in Akmajian (1973), and were also incorporated into Jackendoff's (1972) wide ranging and interesting treatment of focus and presupposition. A "mixed theory" of anaphora, adopted in this thesis in Chapter 4, was later argued for in Bresnan (1971) and Hankamer and Sag (1976), who presented interesting evidence for the hypothesis that ϕ-anaphora (such as ellipsis) is syntactically controlled and derived transformationally, while non-null anaphors (such as it in do it) are base generated and must be interpreted.

Not all the ideas in this dissertation have fared so well. The analysis of cleft and pseudo-cleft sentences, in particular, has remained controversial, and significant criticisms and modifications of the approach taken here have appeared in Higgins (1973), Emonds (1976) and Gundel (1977), among others.

In any event, it is very gratifying to have seen over the past eight years that many of the issues and ideas contained in this dissertation, even if controversial, have continued to be of interest to linguists pursuing new lines of research.

Adrian Akmajian
Tucson, Arizona
July, 1978

References

Akmajian, A.   (1973)   "The Role of Focus in the Interpretation of Anaphoric Expressions", in Anderson, S. R. and P. Kiparsky, eds., (1973), A Festschrift for Morris Halle, Holt, Rinehart and Winston, New York.

Bresnan, J.   (1971)   "A Note on the Notion 'Identity of Sense Anaphora'", Linguistic Inquiry 2, pp. 589-597.

Bresnan, J.   (1978)   "A Realistic Transformational Grammar", in Halle, M.,J. Bresnan, and G. A. Miller, eds., (1978), Linguistic Theory and Psychological Reality, MIT Press, Cambridge, Mass.

Chomsky, N.   (1968)   "Deep Structure, Surface Structure, and Semantic Interpretation", in Jakobovits, L. A. and D. D. Steinberg, eds., (1971), Semantics: An Interdisciplinary Reader in Philosophy, Psychology, Linguistics and Anthropology, Cambridge University Press, Cambridge, England.

Chomsky, N. and H. Lasnik (1977) "Filters and Control",
    Linguistic Inquiry 8, pp. 425-504.

Emonds, J. (1976) A Transformational Approach to English
    Syntax, Academic Press, New York.

Gundel, J. K. (1977) "Where do Cleft Sentences Come From?",
    Language 53, pp. 543-559.

Hankamer, J. and I. Sag (1976) "Deep and Surface Anaphora",
    Linguistic Inquiry 7, pp. 391-428.

Higgins, F. R. (1973) The Pseudo-Cleft Construction in Eng-
    lish, Ph.D. dissertation, M.I.T., Cambridge, Mass.

Jackendoff, R. S. (1969) Some Rules of Semantic Interpretation
    for English, Ph.D. dissertation, M.I.T., Cambridge, Mass.

Jackendoff, R. S. (1972) Semantic Interpretation in Generative
    Grammar, MIT Press, Cambridge, Mass.

ASPECTS OF THE GRAMMAR OF FOCUS IN ENGLISH

by

Adrian Akmajian

B.A., University of Arizona

(1966)

SUBMITTED IN PARTIAL FULFILLMENT
OF THE REQUIREMENTS FOR THE
DEGREE OF DOCTOR OF
PHILOSOPHY

at the

MASSACHUSETTS INSTITUTE OF
TECHNOLOGY

August, 1970

Signature of Author..
Department of Foreign   August 24, 1970
Literatures and Linguistics

Certified by..
Thesis Supervisor

Accepted by..
Chairman, Departmental Committee
on Graduate Students

3

ACKNOWLEDGEMENTS

I have benefited greatly over the past several years
from discussions with various friends, colleagues, and teachers
concerning the issues dealt with in this thesis. Specifically, I wish to express my gratitude to the following people
for particularly helpful comments and suggestions: Stephen R.
Anderson, Joan Bresnan, Peter Culicover, Joseph Emonds, Bob
Faraci, Michael Helke, Irwin Howard, Jerry Katz, Bill Leben,
David Vetter, and George Williams. I have tried to credit
them where I have used their ideas; unfortunately, I must
accept full responsibility for all wrong and foolish thinking
contained in the following pages.

Both David Perlmutter and John R. Ross have provided me
with excellent suggestions in the revision of an earlier
draft of this thesis. Bruce Fraser, of the Language Research
Foundation (Cambridge), has provided continual encouragement,
and I am grateful to him for putting up with hours of arguing
about various issues. Special thanks go to Ray Jackendoff,
who has always been a constant source of stimulating ideas.

My deepest gratitude goes to three teachers, from whom

I have benefited immeasurably: to Kenneth Hale, from whom I first took courses in linguistics; to Noam Chomsky, whose lectures and writings have stimulated the work in this thesis; and finally, to Morris Halle, under whom I wrote this thesis, who has provided so many hours of detailed, critical discussion.

The research contained in this thesis was supported in part by a grant from the TEC Company of Tokyo, Japan, to the Language Research Foundation, Cambridge, Massachusetts.

Finally, let me publicly apologize to Patty Regan and Katrina Streiff for subjecting them to the less than stimulating task of typing this thesis.

TABLE OF CONTENTS

Acknowledgements 3

Introduction 10

Chapter 1

The Syntactic Derivation of Pseudo-Cleft Sentences

1. Terminology 18

2. Motivations for a Transformational Analysis of
   Pseudo-Cleft Sentences. 21

3. Transformational Theories of Pseudo-Cleft
   Sentences 27

   3.1. The Extraction Theory. 27

   3.2. The Deletion Theory. 30

4. Pseudo-Cleft Sentences as Base Generated
   Structures. 32

5. Syntactic Motivation for a Dual Source· 38

   5.1. Consequences of the Existence of a
        Source in the Base 44

6. Extraction or Deletion? 54

   6.1. Evidence from Distribution of Pro-Forms. . . 56

   6.2. Arguments from the Derivation of Cleft
        Sentences. 66

7. The Embedded Question Alternative 71

8. Summary 81

Footnotes to Chapter 1 83

Chapter 2

The Syntactic Derivation of Cleft Sentences

1. Deriving Cleft Sentences from Pseudo-Cleft
   Sentences . . . . Page 104

2. On Motivating Transformational Rules. 106

3. Evidence for the Proposal 107

   3.1. Evidence from Verb Agreement Patterns. . . . 107

   3.2. Evidence from Reflexive Agreements in
        the Clause 117

   3.3. Reflexives in Focus Position 124

   3.4. Evidence from Idiomatic Reflexive
        Constructions. 127

4. The Deep Structure Source for Cleft Sentences . . 130

5. Evidence from the Derivation of Prepositional
   Phrases 133

6. Restrictions on Items Which Can Appear in
   Focus Position. 141

7. Further Extensions. 145

8. Summary 147

Footnotes to Chapter 2 148

Chapter 3

The Semantic Interpretation of Clefted Sentences
and the Semantic Representation of Focus-Presupposition
Relations

1. Objectives. 160

2. Basic Factors in the Interpretation of
   Clefted Sentences 162

2.1. Specificational vs. Predicational. . . Page 162

2.2. Referential vs. Non-Referential. 166

2.3. Further Distinguishing Features. 168

3. Semantic Ambiguity in Clefted Sentences 174

4. The Semantic Interpretation of Clefted
   Sentences 182

4.1. Deep Structure Considerations. 183

4.2. Surface Structure Considerations 188

5. 'Focus' and 'Presupposition'. 189

5.1. The Linguistic Significance of the Notions
     'Focus' and 'Presupposition' 194

5.1.1. The Notion of Focus and the Structure
       of Discourse. 194

5.1.2. Scope of Logical Elements 203

6. The Semantic Notation for Focus and
   Presupposition. 213

6.1. Justification for Proposed Semantic
     Notation 221

6.1.1. Focus as 'Novel' Information. . . . 222

6.1.2. Logical Scope and Attraction
       to Focus. 224

6.2. Intonation and Semantic Representation . . . 238

6.2.1. Contradictive vs. Conclusive. . . . 238

7. Concluding Remarks on Clefted Sentences 250

8. A Note on Syntactic Representation vs.
   Semantic Representation 251

Footnotes to Chapter 3 254

Chapter 4

Focus and the Interpretation of Anaphoric Expressions

1. Focus and Anaphora. . . . . Page 268

2. An Interpretive Principle: Pairing of Foci. . . . 272

    2.1. Sentences with More Than One Focus 275

    2.2. Shifting Intonation Centers. 276

    2.3. Combining Presuppositions. 278

    2.4. Filtering Deviant Cases. 281

    2.5. Cases with No Pairing of Foci. 284

3. Ross's Objections 287

    3.1. 'Sluicing' 287

        3.1.1. Syntactic Arguments in Favor of
        Sluicing. 288

    3.2. The Transformational Approach:
    Syntactic Deletion 291

    3.3. "Sloppy Identity" 295

        3.3.1. Defects in the Notion of Sloppy
        Identity. 296

4. An Interpretive Approach to Pronoun Ambiguities . 301

    4.1. Intonation and Pronoun Ambiguities 302

        4.1.1. Perceptual Cues for Intonation
        Peaks 305

    4.2. Cases with Two or More Anaphoric Expressions 307

5. Deletion Rules and Interpretive Rules 309

    5.1. Compatibility of Deletion Rules and
    Interpretive Rules 311

5.2. Evidence That Deletion is Not Meaning-
     Preserving . . . . Page 314

6. Summary 316

Footnotes to Chapter 4 318

Bibliography 331

Biographical Note. 335

INTRODUCTION

The central purpose of this study is to present specific
syntactic and semantic analyses within a particular area of
English grammar, namely that which we can label as the 'grammar of focus'. This term is intended to delineate an area of
grammar which has to do with the partitioning of a sentence
into portions which are 'prominent', 'novel', 'emphasized',
and so forth, as opposed to portions which are 'presupposed',
'assumed', or 'anaphoric'.

In particular, this area of grammar has to do with sets
of sentences such as the following:

(1) What caused the greatest devastation in the 14th
    century was the plague.

(2) It was the plague that caused the greatest devasta-
    tion in the 14th century.

(3) THE PLAGUE caused the greatest devastation in the
    14th century.

Such sentences are intuitively judged as being quite similar
and related in various ways. Each of the sentences above has
the same constituent as its _focus_, namely the constituent
the plague. This constituent, in each sentence, is understood

as being semantically prominent, or novel (in a sense made more precise in Chapter 3), with respect to the surrounding material. The remainder of the material in these sentences is said to be 'presupposed' or non-prominent.

In this study we investigate the syntactic and semantic inter-relationships which hold among sets of sentences such as (1), (2), and (3). The most important task of this thesis is to present concrete and specific grammatical analysis of these grammatical inter-relations. The work presented in this study falls naturally into two parts.

In the first half of the thesis we present a syntactic analysis of pseudo-cleft and cleft sentences. In Chapter 1, the syntactic derivation of pseudo-cleft sentences is discussed. We attempt to show that pseudo-cleft sentences (such as (1)) are syntactically related to non-clefted sentences (such as (3)), and that a theory of pseudo-cleft sentences must provide for deep structure representations of pseudo-cleft sentences which incorporate the phrase markers for the corresponding non-clefted sentences. In this regard, we follow Bach and Peters [1968] and Chomsky [1967]. While any theory must express a syntactic relation holding between pseudo-cleft sentences and non-clefted sentences, we go on to argue that pseudo-cleft sentences also derive from a second, independent source within the grammar, namely, a base expansion of NP-be-NP. Thus, it emerges that pseudo-cleft sentences are in some ways syntactically independent from non-clefted sentences, and we present positive evidence for this position. Finally, two transformational theories of pseudo-cleft sentences are compared (i.e. that of Bach and Peters [1968] and that of Chomsky [1967]), and we argue in favor of so-called 'extraction analyses'.

In Chapter 2, we argue that pseudo-cleft sentences and cleft sentences (i.e. (1) and (2)) must be syntactically related. It is proposed that cleft sentences derive syntactically from pseudo-cleft sentences by a rule which extraposes the initial clause of the pseudo-cleft sentence. Thus, it emerges that the syntactic inter-relations holding between sentences (1), (2), and (3) are expressed by deriving (1) from (3) (in the sense that the phrase marker for (3) is incorporated into the deep structure phrase marker for (1)); and by deriving (2) from (1).

Throughout the first half of the thesis, the evidence presented for specific syntactic analyses is formal in nature, i.e. it is evidence from the formal shape of sentences, rather than evidence from meaning, as such. In particular, the evidence consists in arguments from syntactic distribution, for example, arguments dealing with syntactic agreement patterns, distribution of derived phrases, and so forth.

In the second half of the thesis we investigate the semantic inter-relationships holding between pseudo-cleft, cleft, and non-clefted sentences. In Chapter 3 we begin with a consideration of semantic ambiguities in pseudo-cleft sentences, concluding that there are no semantic ambiguities which can be associated with the dual source for pseudo-cleft sentences. We then proceed to a discussion of the semantic representation of sets of related clefted and non-clefted sentences. The primary task of Chapter 3 is to develop a semantic notation for focus-presupposition relations and to show how sets of sentences such as (1), (2), and (3) are assigned identical focus-presupposition representations within this notation. We follow the general approach first outlined by Chomsky [1969], i.e., an approach in which focus-presupposition relations are determined by semantic interpretive rules operating on the level of (phonetically interpreted) surface structures. It emerges that sets of sentences such as (1), (2), and (3) are assigned identical semantic representations, even though their syntactic deep structure representations are not identical.

Finally, in Chapter 4, we discuss ways in which the semantic notation developed in Chapter 3 can be extended to other parts of the grammar. Specifically, that chapter deals with semantic interpretive principles for anaphoric expressions, and we attempt to show that the notation for focus-presupposition relations plays a crucial role in the interpretation of certain anaphoric expressions.

While the primary purpose of this thesis is to present specific grammatical analysis for a range of data, some of the work presented here has direct bearing on certain theoretical issues of current interest. The theoretical framework adopted in this thesis is that which has been discussed and developed in particular by Chomsky ([1967], [1969], [1970]), Jackendoff ([1969]), and Emonds ([1970]), and which has come to be labeled generally as the 'Interpretive' framework.

There are two specific theoretical assumptions of this particular framework which are of relevance for this study:

I.   There is a level of syntactic deep structure, independent of semantic representation. In particular, this is the level which is formed by the rules of the base, which forms the output of lexical insertion rules, and the input to transformations.

II. The level of syntactic surface structure is available as an input for semantic interpretive rules, and thus the semantic representation of sentences is not defined exclusively by the level of deep structure.

Confirmation of I, above, is found in the derivation of pseudo-cleft sentences. We attempt to show that the pseudo-cleft can derive from two syntactic sources, and further that no ambiguity can be associated with this duality of source. Hence, an unambiguous sentence can derive from two formally distinct deep structures. This is consistent only with a theory in which deep structure representations are distinct from semantic representations. (For recent work dealing with the notion of deep structure, see S.R. Anderson [forthcoming, b] and P. Culicover [1970].)

Notice, incidentally, that the claim that an unambiguous sentence can have more than one deep structure source does not represent a departure from standard transformational theory. For example, within the framework developed by Katz and Postal [1964], it is logically necessary to assign to an ambiguous surface structure more than one deep structure re- presentation (the number of sources being equal to the number of possible sources). This is simply a consequence of the assumption that the semantic interpretation of a sentence must be explicitly and discretely represented in the deep structure phrase marker, and that only this level determines semantic interpretation. However, the converse is not true. Even within the Katz-Postal framework, it is logically possible for an unambiguous surface structure to derive from more than one deep structure, each deep structure source being formally distinct. This is because within that framework the level of syntactic deep structure is distinct from the level of semantic representation, and therefore there exists a logical possibility that semantic interpretive rules can assign the same semantic readings to formally distinct deep structure phrase markers. We argue that this logical possibility is in fact instantiated in the case of pseudo-cleft sentences.

Turning now to theoretical assumption II above, throughout Chapters 3 and 4 we argue for interpretive principles which operate on surface structures. In Chapter 3 we present arguments that focus-presupposition relations must be determined on surface structures: i.e., that the relevant generalizations are surface structural generalizations in the sense that the focus-presupposition relations of a sentence are determined by the surface derived phrase structure of a sentence, as well as various factors of intonation. In Chapter 4 we present arguments that interpretive principles for anaphoric expressions must operate on surface structures as well, since these must make crucial use of focus-presupposition relations.

While the work in this thesis is approached from an Interpretive point of view, it is not our purpose to present negative arguments against other possible alternatives. In particular, this thesis is not intended to constitute a criticism of the theoretical position which is known as "Generative

Semantics" (cf. Lakoff [1969]). It is not clear at this time whether in fact the two approaches represent genuine alternatives or merely variants of some sort (for discussion of this issue, see Chomsky [1970]). Therefore, it must be emphasized that the central purpose of this thesis is to present facts which any theory must account for, and to present analyses which all theories must adopt in some form.

CHAPTER 1

THE SYNTACTIC DERIVATION OF PSEUDO-CLEFT SENTENCES

1. Terminology

We take the term pseudo-cleft to refer to the class of
copula constructions of the following sort:

(1) a. The one Nixon chose was Agnew.

b. The thing which Herman bought was that tarantula.

c. The place where he finally ended up was Berkeley.

d. The time at which John arrived was 5 o'clock.

e. The reason Fillmore sent Perry was to exploit the
Japanese.

f. The way he did that was by using a decoder.

(2) a. Who Nixon chose was Agnew.[1]

b. What Herman bought was that tarantula.

c. Where he finally ended up was in Berkeley.

d. When John arrived was at 5 o'clock.

e. Why Fillmore sent Perry was to exploit the
Japanese.

   f. How he did that was by using a decoder.
The initial relative clauses of (1) have full lexical heads,
while those of (2) do not have lexically realized heads. We
refer to the clauses of (1) as "bound" relatives, and those
of (2) as "free" relatives. In each case we refer to the
post-copular constituent as the <u>focus</u> of the pseudo-cleft,
and the post-copular position as the <u>focus position</u>.

   The essential feature that distinguishes pseudo-cleft
sentences from other copula constructions is that the initial
clause of the pseudo-cleft contains what is essentially a
semantic variable, a semantic 'gap' which must be 'filled' or
specified by the focus item. In this respect, pseudo-cleft
sentences are related to WH questions and their answers,
which also enter into a relation of specification. Notice
that sentences such as those of (1) contain relative clauses
whose heads function as variables ranging over given semantic
classes. Thus, <u>one</u> acts as a variable ranging over the class
of humans, <u>thing</u> ranges over the class of inanimates, and so
forth. In the sentences of (2), the WH words of the free
relatives function as semantic variables, again ranging over
appropriate classes. The focus item must specify a value for
the variable of the clause, and it thus follows that the focus
item must belong to the appropriate semantic class, i.e., the
class represented by the variable.

Related to this is the fact that pseudo-cleft sentences
enter into paraphrase relationships with non-clefted sentences, in the sense that if the variable of the clause were
replaced by the focus item, a well-formed sentence should
result. For example, sentences such as (1) and (2) have
paraphrases of the following sort:[2]

(3) Nixon chose Agnew.

(4) Herman bought that tarantula.

. . .

(This parallelism with non-clefted sentences has in fact been
taken as the central fact to be accounted for in transformational
analyses of pseudo-cleft sentences.) In sum, a
necessary characteristic of the pseudo-cleft is the existence
of a semantic variable (or 'gap') contained in a free or
bound relative. Further, this variable is specified by the
focus item, and in this way the pseudo-cleft is analogous in
function to question-answer pairs.

2. Motivations for a Transformational Analysis of Pseudo-Cleft Sentences

As we have mentioned, grammarians have viewed the parallelism between pseudo-cleft and non-clefted sentences as the central fact to be accounted for in the analysis of pseudo-cleft sentences. For example, Bach and Peters [1968] in presenting their analysis discuss sentences such as:

(5) a. What John counted was the pigeons.

     b. John counted the pigeons.

They note that both sentences are understood to have the same grammatical relations, and that violations of selectional restrictions in one will be matched in the other (e.g., the impossibility of a singular count noun as the object of count). Bach and Peters go on to make the claim that whatever can fit into the frame (6a) can also fit into the frame (6b):

(6) a. What John counted was ____.

     b. John counted ____.

The distribution of items in post-copular position is thus held to be a function of the distribution of these items in non-clefted sentences. Bach and Peters go on to state:

(7) "...it is clear that in any theory with a modicum of explanatory adequacy the most highly valued grammar compatible with these data will assign

to a pseudo-cleft sentence a deep structure containing a phrase marker closely resembling the
deep structure of the corresponding uncleffed
sentence."

Part of the motivation for (7) consists in arguments
from similarity of grammatical relations and selectional
restrictions. However, arguments of a more interesting sort,
which go beyond similarity of grammatical relations, have
also been advanced. The arguments in question are based on
the observation that in certain pseudo-cleft sentences there
is a grammatical dependence, or grammatical connectedness,
between the focus item and the initial clause.

Consider, for example, arguments based on the distribu-
tion of reflexive pronouns, which have been presented by
J.R. Ross [class lectures], and Bach and Peters [1968].
Take the following sentences:

(8) a. What John did was wash $\left\{ \begin{array}{l} \text{himself} \\ \text{*him} \\ \text{*herself} \end{array} \right\}$.

b. What John wants Mary to do is wash $\left\{ \begin{array}{l} \text{*himself} \\ \text{him} \\ \text{herself} \end{array} \right\}$.

(Starred forms indicate impossibility of coreferentiality
with some item in the preceding clause.) The distribution

of reflexive forms in (8a-b) is parallel with the distribution of such forms in non-clefted sentences, such as:

(9) a. John washed $\left\{\begin{array}{l}\text{himself} \\ *\text{him} \\ *\text{herself}\end{array}\right\}$.

  b. John wants Mary to wash $\left\{\begin{array}{l}*\text{himself} \\ \text{him} \\ \text{herself}\end{array}\right\}$.

To capture this fact, analyses proposed so far (Chomsky
[1967], Bach and Peters [1968], J.R. Ross [class lectures],
Emonds [1970]) meet the condition specified in (7), i.e. the
pseudo-cleft deep structure for sentences such as (8) contains
an embedded phrase marker for sentences such as (9). In this
way, such theories express the generalization that the
distribution of reflexives in pseudo-cleft and non-clefted
sentences is governed by the same principles. In this sense,
then, we use the term 'grammatical connectedness': the
appearance of reflexive pronouns in pseudo-cleft sentences
such as those of (8) is not arbitrary or independent of anything else within these sentences. Rather, the distribution
of such forms is 'governed' by the initial clauses. To
capture this fact, a transformational analysis which meets
condition (7) is required.[3]

  If we were to assume otherwise, i.e., that pseudo-cleft

sentences bear no transformational relationship to non-clefted sentences, it would then be costly to account for the facts manifested in (8). First we would note that the reflexivization rule (or principle) which operates within single clauses could not operate on sentences such as (8), since the reflexive pronoun is dominated by a different $\underline{S}$ node than its antecedent. Therefore, some extension of the rule would be necessary. However, such an extension of the rule would be merely a restatement of the rule with some ad-hoc provision added to allow reflexives to appear in pseudo-cleft sentences (i.e. to allow the copula to intervene between the reflexive and its antecedent). This is the case simply because the facts of (8) and (9) are completely parallel.

Such distributional arguments can be extended in various ways. For example, consider the interaction of the distribution of reflexive forms with the distribution of derived phrases in focus position:

(10) a. What John is is <u>eager to please</u> (himself).

b. What John is is <u>easy to please</u> (*himself).

We note that derived surface phrases may appear in focus position, which in itself presents problems for a theory which would generate pseudo-cleft sentences completely independently of non-clefted sentences.[4] Further, one would be faced with the problem of accounting for the fact that the reflexive may appear in (10a) but not in (10b). However, theories which adhere to principle (7) have a natural account for sentences such as those of (10), since the pseudo-cleft deep structure would incorporate the phrase markers for the following non-clefted sentences:

    (11) a. John is eager to please (himself).

        b. John is easy to please (*himself).

These would be represented with phrase markers of roughly the following form:

    (12) a. [John be eager [John please $\left\{ \begin{array}{c} \text{PRO} \\ \text{John} \end{array} \right\}$]]

        b. [[PRO please John] be easy]

These would be first subject to operations which would map them onto sentences such as (11), and these in turn would be subject to some sort of clefting operation. In this way, the facts of (10) and (11) would be accounted for in a unitary fashion. For such reasons, then, a transformational analysis of pseudo-cleft sentences is motivated.[5]

    The fundamental claim embodied by a transformational analysis is that restrictions on pseudo-cleft sentences are parallel with restrictions on non-clefted sentences. This claim, however, needs to be qualified somewhat at the outset, in that not all restrictions on pseudo-clefts are related to restrictions in non-clefted sentences. In particular, since

pseudo-cleft sentences contain relative clauses, they are
bound to restrictions on relatives. For example, consider
the following:

(13) a. *What I forced was Bill to leave.

b. *What I forced Bill was to leave.

c. What I forced Bill to do was leave.

The ungrammaticality of sentences such as (13a) and (13b) has
nothing to do with the specific transformational derivation
of pseudo-cleft sentences, but is a consequence of the fact
that in any event there are no relative clauses of the
following form:

(14) a. *What I forced.

b. *What I forced Bill.

The facts of (13) and (14) are naturally related to facts
concerning the distribution of pro-forms:

(15) a. *I forced something.

b. *I forced Bill something.

Therefore, we must recognize at the outset that not all
restrictions on pseudo-cleft sentences can be related to
restrictions on non-clefted sentences.

3. Transformational Theories of Pseudo-Cleft Sentences

3.1. The Extraction Theory. The transformational analysis of pseudo-cleft sentences which we adopt in this study is that proposed by Chomsky [1967] and Emonds [1970], which we refer to as the Extraction Theory.[6] The essential feature of this analysis is that the focus position is empty at the deep structure level, and is filled by the extraction transformation, which operates on an embedded clause. For example, the deep structure for sentences such as (16) would be (17) (taken from Chomsky [1967]):

(16) a. What John read was a book about himself.

b. What John did was read a book about himself.

(17)

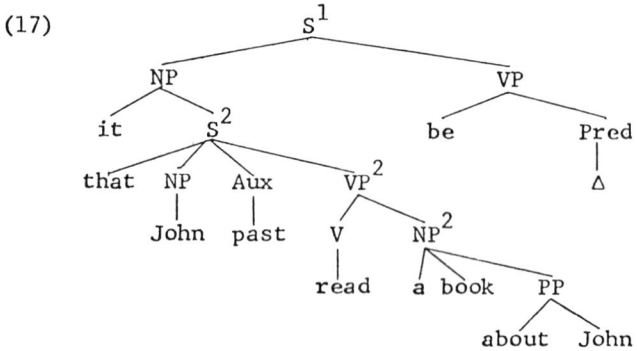

(The symbol Pred is here used merely as an abbreviation for the various category nodes which can appear in this position.)[7] The rule which forms the pseudo-cleft sentence is a rule which

extracts a major constituent of the embedded sentence (e.g.
S, NP, VP, PP), and places this constituent in the position
of the empty Δ, leaving behind an appropriate pro-form in the
place of the extracted constituent.

To take an example, let us consider the derivation of
the sentences of (16). First, on the level of S^2 of (17),
the reflexivization rule (or principle) operates to 'reflex-
ivize' the second occurrence of the NP John, thus giving for
S^2 John read a book about himself. On the S^1 cycle two rules
of relevance must apply, namely the Extraction Rule and then
WH-Fronting, in that order. For (16a), the extraction rule
applies to S^2 by extracting NP^2, placing it in the position
of the empty predicate Δ, and leaving in its place a pro-form
what (i.e. WH + it). This leaves us with the following
intermediate structure:

(18) [[it [that-John-do-WH+it]] be
$_{VP}$[read a book about himself]$_{VP}$]

Again, the WH-fronting rule applies on the initial clause,
forming (16b).

It should be remarked that we assume a theory of
relativization discussed by Emonds [1970] and Bresnan [1970].
Within this theory, it is assumed that the introductory that
of relative clauses is the complementizer that which intro-
duces propositional complements of certain verbs (cf. Bresnan

[1970] for discussion). Secondly, following Emonds [1970], it is assumed that relativization is carried out in stages, in two possible ways. One possibility is that the NP to be relativized (which is marked by WH) is first pronominalized. After it has been pronominalized, the WH fronting rule moves it to the front of the sentence, _replacing_ the complementizer _that_. The second possibility is that the NP to be relativized is simply deleted, resulting in relative clauses introduced by _that_. As an example of a derivation of relative clauses, consider the following (from Emonds [1970]):

(20) a. Deep Structure

The friend [that-I spoke to WH-friend] drove away.

b. Removal of NP by relativization, with optional pronoun left behind

A. The friend [that I spoke to WH-him] drove away.

B. The friend [that I spoke to   ] drove away.

c. WH-fronting in A of either NP or PP dominating pronominalized NP

A. The friend [who I spoke to] drove away.

B. The friend [to whom I spoke] drove away.

Note that the operation of the Extraction Rule produces similar results, as Emonds points out. That is, the rule removes an NP from an embedded clause, leaving behind a pro-form, which we assume is marked as [+PRO, +WH]. The pro-form

is then fronted, and replaces the complementizer <u>that</u>.
Furthermore, there are cases (which we discuss later) where
the Extraction Rule removes a constituent from the embedded
clause and leaves no pro-form behind, leaving a clause introduced by the complementizer <u>that</u>.

The Extraction Rule itself must be stated as a schema,
since it extracts any major constituent of the embedded
sentence:

(21) Extraction Rule:

$$[\ _S[\ X - A - Y \ ]_S \ \text{be} \ [\ \Delta \ ] \ ] \ \rightarrow$$
$$[\ _S[\ X - [+PRO,+WH] - Y \ ]_S \ \text{be} \ [\ A \ ] \ ]$$

<u>A</u> must be a constituent; however, this condition need not be
stated on this particular rule, since we restrict movement
rules in general to operating only on constituents. Hence,
this general condition insures that only constituents will
be affected.

3.2. The Deletion Theory. Another analysis of pseudo-
cleft sentences which has been proposed recently is that of
Bach and Peters [1968] and J.R. Ross [class lectures], which
we refer to as the Deletion Theory. The essential feature of

this theory is that the predicate position is filled in deep structure with a full sentence, a portion of which must be deleted to leave behind the focus constituent. For example, consider the following deep structure:

(22)

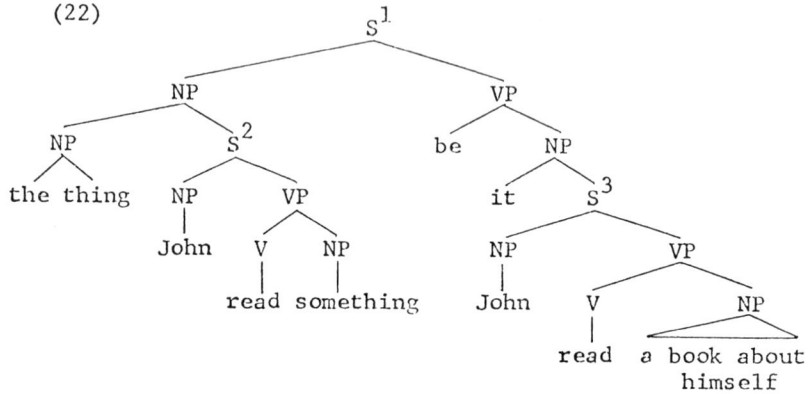

In this analysis, there is an initial bound relative (with thing as its head), with an NP dominating a sentence in focus position. The rule which forms the pseudo-cleft is a deletion rule, which deletes all elements of S^3 which are identical with the non-pro-form elements of S^2. Bach and Peters state the rule thus [1968, p. 9]:

(23)

the thing [$_S$ that X Y]$_S$ Aux be it # [$_S$ X' NP Y']$_S$ #

1	2	3	4	5	6	7	8	9
1	2	3	4	Ø	Ø	7	Ø	Ø

where: 2 = 6
3 = 8

In the case of (22), the items John and read of S^3 are deleted
under identity with these items in S^2.

We will discuss the relative merits of the Extraction
and Deletion theories in section 6. The point to be made
here is that there is good motivation for a transformational
theory of pseudo-cleft sentences which meets condition (7)
(i.e. which incorporates into the pseudo-cleft deep structure
the phrase marker for the corresponding non-clefted sentence),
and that both the Extraction and Deletion theories meet this
condition.

4. Pseudo-Cleft Sentences as Base-Generated Structures

We have attempted to show that a theory of pseudo-cleft
sentences must allow for a transformational derivation of
the sorts discussed in the last section. We will point out
here that pseudo-cleft sentences have also a second source
within the grammar, and that there is no non-ad hoc way of
preventing pseudo-cleft sentences from deriving from two
sources. We refer here to pseudo-cleft sentences as base-
generated copula constructions.

Among the copula constructions in English, there are, in particular, constructions such as the following:

(24) a. Clark Kent is Superman.

b. The man I know is the man who robbed the bank.

c. My problem is my low income.

The grammar must provide a source for such sentences, and there is no simpler source than the basic structure [NP - be - NP]. This syntactic structure is also the source for sentences such as:

(25) a. He is a doctor.

b. He is a fool.

(The difference in interpretation between sentences such as (24) and (25) is discussed in Chapter 3.)

If constructions such as (24) are basic structures, then there is no way to prevent pseudo-cleft sentences from being generated in the base; for example, pseudo-cleft sentences such as:

(26) What I cooked was the spaghetti.

Both underlined phrases are dominated by the node NP, and can appear in positions where any NP can. In particular, free relatives such as the initial clause of (26) appear in all NP environments:

(27) a. I threw away what John cooked.

b. What John cooked was believed to have been

eaten by Bill.

c. What he cooked was lumpy and cold.

d. What I threw out was what John cooked.

Therefore, if the base contains the expansion [NP - be - NP],

then pseudo-cleft sentences are generated by the base.[8]

This situation raises certain questions as to how

deviant sentences are to be blocked. Compare, for example,

the following two sentences, both of which could be syntacti-

cally generated by the base structure [NP - be - NP]:

(28) a. What I cooked yesterday was Hemingway's

favorite Italian dish.

b. *What I cooked yesterday was Hemingway's suicide.

We ask, then, how sentences such as (28b) are to be blocked.

Within a transformational derivation, of course, sentences

such as (28b) could not be generated, since (28b) would con-

tain in its deep structure a phrase marker for the deviant

sentence:

(29)   *I cooked Hemingway's suicide.

Because of violations in selectional restrictions, sentences

such as (29), and therefore (28b), are blocked. Thus, the

transformational analysis relates the ungrammaticality of

(28b) with that of (29).

We must note, however, that this explanation won't do

for other cases, where the transformational analysis fails to capture certain parallels. Specifically, that analysis fails to capture the similarity bwtween (28b) and the following, (30):

    (30)   *The food was Hemingway's suicide.

Sentences such as (30), obviously, do not undergo a clefting operation, but must be marked as deviant by the grammar in any event. Furthermore, whatever mechanism marks (30) as deviant will also mark (28b) as deviant.

    The deviance of (28b) and (30) has to do with the fact that the semantic composition of the two NP's connected by the copula is in conflict. Consider, for example:

    (31)   *The man over there is the woman that I know.

We understand this sentence to be odd in certain ways, and we know that it fails as a specificational statement.[9] This is due to the contradiction arising in equating a noun phrase with the semantic information [Male] with a noun phrase with the semantic information [NonMale]. The noun phrases in a specificational statement must necessarily 'agree' in their semantic features. Specifically, the noun phrases in question must be non-distinct with respect to all those semantic features which play a role in selectional restrictions.[10]

    To take the example of (30), note that the NP food has the semantic marking for concreteness, while the NP

<u>Hemingway's suicide</u> has the semantic marking for abstractness.
The distinction concrete/abstract plays a role in selectional
restrictions, and therefore the two NPs in a specificational
statement must agree with respect to this feature. Since
they do not in (30), the sentence is ruled out.

We should emphasize here that features which play no
role in selectional restrictions need not agree:

    (32) A man that I saw yesterday is the man who robbed
          the bank.

Even though one NP is syntactically indefinite and the other
syntactically definite, this is a semantically well-formed
sentence. Note, in addition, that the syntactic distinction
indefinite/definite plays no role in selectional restrictions.

Returning to sentence (28b), we now note that it can be
blocked in just the manner that (30) is blocked. Let us
assume that the deep representation of the <u>what</u>-clause of
(28b) is [I - cooked - [+PRO,+WH]]. Following Katz and
Postal [1964, pp. 81-84], we assume that the reading of a
pro-form is composed of whatever semantic information it may
possess as an independent lexical item, <u>along with</u> semantic
information which it acquires from the context in which it
is found. That is, Katz and Postal propose that by a general
convention within the theory of grammar, pro-forms acquire
the semantic information projected by the selectional

features of the items with which they enter into selectional
relations. Thus, the verb cook, in (28b), projects onto the
pro-form (something) the semantic features specified by the
selectional restrictions for possible objects of cook. When
the pro-form is fronted, it is thus marked with the semantic
features common to all possible objects of the verb cook.

This is necessary for reasons completely independent of
the question of blocking pseudo-cleft sentences. For example,
consider sentences such as:

    (33) a. I ate what John cooked.

        b. *I ate what John said.

As Joan Bresnan [1970] points out, in free relatives the
element what must satisfy selectional restrictions within the
relative itself, as well as within the matrix sentence. Thus,
in (33b), what is marked with those semantic features common
to all possible objects of say; however, in the matrix sentence these features violate the selectional restrictions of
the verb eat. If we assume that semantic features are
associated with whole phrases, as well as single lexical
categories (cf. Jackendoff [1966], Chomsky [1967], McCawley
[1968]), then the free relative as a whole takes on the
semantic feature composition of the pro-form what. This in
turn derives its semantic content from the elements with
which it enters into selectional relations. Thus, a phrase

such as what I cooked takes on, as a whole, the semantic

features common to all possible objects of the verb cook.

In this way, (28b) is completely parallel with (30)

since the NPs what I cooked and the food share semantic

features common to all possible objects of the verb cook.

This will mean, then, that what I cooked will be marked, as

a whole, as semantically concrete, while the phrase

Hemingway's suicide is marked as semantically abstract.

Therefore, (28b) is marked as deviant for the same reason as

(30).

5. Syntactic Motivation for a Dual Source

So far we have seen that a transformational derivation

of pseudo-cleft sentences is required, and further that the

base also generates pseudo-cleft sentences. It should be

noted that there is no non-ad hoc way to prevent this

situation. It would greatly complecate the grammar to

attempt to restrict the base in such a manner as to prevent

pseudo-cleft sentences from being generated, since (a subset

of) pseudo-cleft sentences are permissible expansions of the

base rule [NP - be - NP]. In this section we note that

there is some positive evidence for a dual source for pseudo-
cleft sentences, in that such a dualism accounts for certain
syntactic facts. The set of facts we consider here involves
the rule of There-Insertion.

If we assume that the rule of There-Insertion (cf. J.R.
Ross [1967], Chomsky [1967], Emonds [1970]) is cyclic, then
there is a class of pseudo-cleft sentences which cannot be
derived in the transformational theories outlined above (or
any transformational theory which posits a non-clefted sentence embedded in the deep structure of the clefted sentence).
Consider in this regard the following:

(34) What there was in the car was $\left\{\begin{array}{l}\text{the jack you gave me}\\\text{my hat}\end{array}\right\}$.

In pre-copular position the clause contains existential
there; however, in post-copular position there is a definite
noun phrase. There is no corresponding non-clefted sentence
for (34), since There-Insertion is restricted to operating on
indefinite noun phrases:

(35) *There was $\left\{\begin{array}{l}\text{the jack you gave me}\\\text{my hat}\end{array}\right\}$ in the car.

Sentences such as (34) cannot be derived in either the
Extraction or Deletion theories, for differing reasons.

Consider first the Extraction Theory. The presumed
source for (34) would have to be the following:

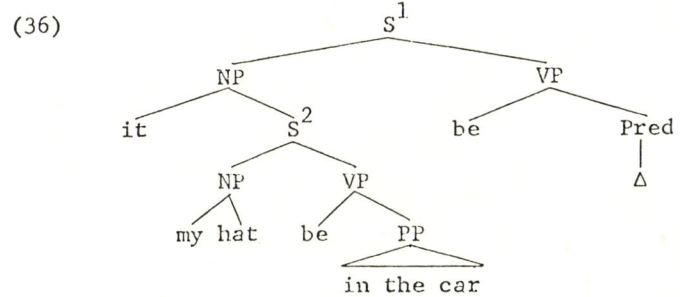

(36)

If the There-Insertion rule is cyclic, it may operate on S^2 if its conditions are met. **However,** note that in S^2 of (36), the conditions for There-Insertion are not met: there may not replace the definite noun phrase my hat. The rule fails to apply and on the S^1 cycle the extraction rule may apply. The only sentence which could be derived would be:

(37) What was in the car was my hat.

which is the result of extracting the NP my hat. However, the version of the sentence with there, as in (34), could not be derived.

Note, by the way, that there is good reason to suppose that the There-Insertion rule is in fact cyclic. Consider examples such as:

(38) There was believed to have been an explosion.

Such examples show that once there has been inserted it behaves just as any other noun phrase with respect to trans-formations, such as Passive and Raising. Since Passive is a cyclic rule, and since it may operate on there, There-

Insertion must also be cyclic. (For further discussion, see
Emonds [1970].)

Consider now the Deletion Theory. It cannot derive
sentences such as (34), since the application of There-
Insertion in the leftmost clause destroys the conditions on
identity required for the deletion rule to apply. The presumed source for (34) within this theory would be:

(39)

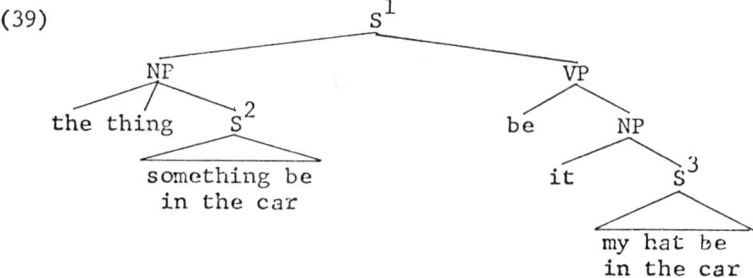

Assuming that There-Insertion may apply in relative clauses
with full heads,[11] we would derive, after application of
this rule, the following:

(40)

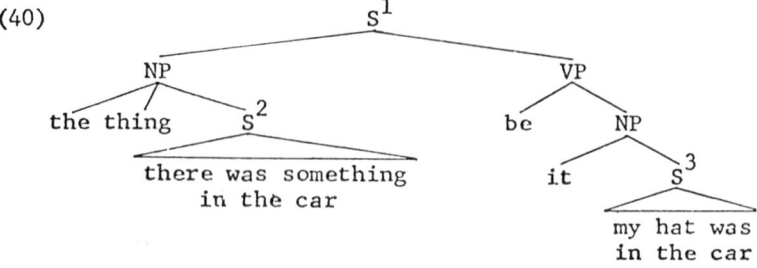

Note, however, that the application of There-Insertion has
destroyed the identity conditions for the Deletion Rule. In

order to derive the noun phrase my hat in post-copular

position, it is necessary to delete was in the car in S^3.

But there is no portion of S^2 identical to S^3 with respect to

this, since in S^2 we have was something in the car. Further-

more, There-Insertion has added the morpheme there to S^2,

which is not found in S^3. Thus, There-Insertion, with its

addition of the morpheme there along with the concomitant

change in word order effected by the rule, creates conditions

such that the deletion rule can no longer apply. Thus, sen-

tences such as (34) are not derivable within either of the

transformational theories.

Sentences such as (34), however, are derivable in the

base source for pseudo-cleft sentences. Consider the follow-

ing deep source:

(41)

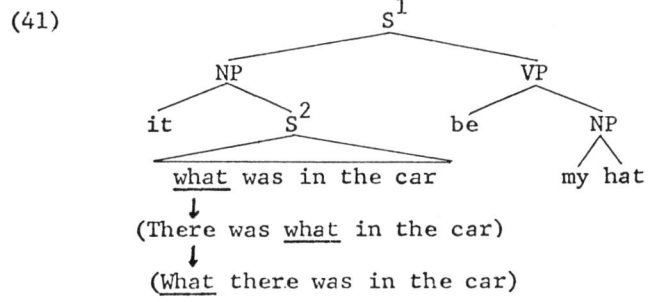

In S^2 of (41), the pro-form represented by what is assigned

semantic features projected by the items with which it enters

into selectional relations. Thus, in a locative statement

(i.e. <u>was in the car</u>) the pro-form must be assigned features
indicating that it is semantically concrete (i.e. something
capable of occupying space). If the post-copular NP is also
marked with such features, the sentence is good. If the
post-copular NP is not marked with such features, the sentence
must be marked as deviant, just as the following are marked
as deviant:

(42) a. *The theory of grammar was in the car.

b. *The item in the car was the theory of grammar.
As before, as long as the features which play a role in
selectional restrictions agree, sentences derived from
structures such as (41) are marked well-formed, and thus the
base can derive sentences such as (34). This case, then,
provides positive evidence in favor of a second source for
pseudo-cleft sentences.[12]

In our discussion of the transformational derivation for
pseudo-cleft sentences, we noted that the primary motivation
for such analyses involved certain distributional facts,
namely, that the distribution of post-copular items is, in
certain cases, a function of the distribution of these items
in non-clefted sentences. With reflexives, for example, we
noted that the conditions for the distribution of reflexive
pronouns in pseudo-cleft sentences were just the conditions
for the distribution of reflexives in non-clefted sentences.

We wish to derive pseudo-clefts in such a way that the principles which govern reflexive coreferentiality patterns in
non-clefted sentences also account for the distribution of
reflexives in pseudo-clefts. In this manner, a transformational analysis is motivated. On the other hand, the case
with There-Insertion is a case in which the distribution of
post-copular items is <u>not</u> a function of the distribution of
these items in non-clefted sentences, and in this sense the
pre-copular and post-copular items are independent (providing,
of course, that the semantic features agree).

5.1. Consequences of the Existence of a Source in the
Base. We should make clear here the logical consequences of
this situation. That is, a certain criterion is used to
establish a transformational analysis of pseudo-cleft sentences, namely, what we have termed 'grammatical connectedness'. If, on the other hand, it is claimed that a certain
class of pseudo-cleft sentences can be generated <u>only</u> in the
base, it should be the case that this particular class of
sentences does not manifest any properties of grammatical
connectedness of the sort which motivates a transformational
analysis.

The case under consideration here is one in which the
initial clause of the pseudo-cleft contains an existential
there, while in focus position there is a syntactically
definite NP. It is argued that this cannot derive from
either transformational source discussed above, but we note
that sentences of this specific sort are generated by the
base. Since it is maintained that sentences of this specific
sort are generated only by the base, then it should be the
case that such sentences do not display dependencies across
the copula which would argue for a transformational analysis
of the sort sketched out above. A specific counterexample
to this position would be one in which a pseudo-cleft sentence contains there in the initial clause, a definite NP in
focus position, and yet displays grammatical dependencies
across the copula.

J.R. Ross has suggested to me that sentences with re-
flexive possessives appear to constitute such counterexamples.
For example, consider a sentence such as the following (from
J.R. Ross):

(43) What there was next to Bill was his own pistol.
The focus phrase in this case, his own pistol, contains the
so-called reflexive possessive, own. If it is the case that
reflexive possessives are governed by the same principles
that govern reflexive pronouns -- i.e., if the antecedent of

a reflexive possessive must be in the same simplex sentence --
then examples such as (43) would argue against generating
such pseudo-cleft sentences in the base. The reason, just as
with sentences such as (8), is that generating such sentences
in the base would complicate the rule or principle which
determines the antecedent of a reflexive possessive. In (43)
the possessive is in the higher sentence, while its antecedent is in the embedded sentence; if, in general, the
antecedent of such a possessive must be in the same simplex
S, then (43) would constitute a special case which would
require some special statement. Just as with the sentences
of (8), sentence (43) would argue for a transformational
derivation. This, then, is the general form a counterexample
would take.

However, if we examine this particular case, we note
that it does not, in fact, constitute a counterexample, since
the antecedent of a reflexive possessive need not be in the
same simplex S. For example, consider the following:

(44) a. John denied that he ever saw a gun, but his
        own pistol was lying on the table.

     b. Even though Mary looks down on people who
        haven't finished their theses, her own thesis
        is far from complete.

In both cases, the antecedent of the reflexive possessive is

dominated by a different S node, and in (44b) the antecedent
is within a subordinate clause. Such examples show that the
reflexive possessive is not governed by the same principles
which govern reflexive pronouns and thus sentences such as
(43) do not represent cases which require special extension
of the principles which determine the antecedents of reflexive possessives. [13]

Similar examples can be constructed with other sorts of
anaphoric expressions. For example, sentences such as the
following might be raised as putative counterexamples:

(45)   What there was next to Bill$_i$ was $\left\{\begin{array}{c} \text{that} \\ \text{the} \end{array}\right\}$

photograph of himself$_i$ which was taken last summer.
In the initial clause there is an occurrence of there, and
the focus NP is definite. Further, there is an anaphoric
item in the focus NP which is coreferential with an item in
the initial clause. Given that the coreferentiality relation
extends 'across the copula', this might be construed as the
sort of grammatical connectedness which motivates a transformational analysis. This would be the case only if it
could be shown that (45) represents a special case, i.e. a
deviance from otherwise general principles of coreferentiality. This would be a case analogous to that represented by
the sentences of (8), in which the pattern of coreferentiality

in the pseudo-cleft is completely parallel with the pattern found in non-clefted sentences. If (45) is generated in the base, would it not then involve an ad hoc extension of otherwise general principles for assigning coreferentiality?

Before answering this, it should be noted that this particular sort of example is not restricted to cases which involve existential <u>there</u>, as we have been discussing. David Perlmutter has suggested to me that such sentences constitute putative counterexamples to the general claim that pseudo-cleft sentences are generated in the base. For example, consider the following (from Perlmutter):

(46) a. What $Bill_i$ read was a book about $himself_i$.

   b. *What $Bill_i$ read was a book about him_i.

If sentence (45) is generated by the base, as we claim, then the sentences of (46) would also have to be generated by the base, since they are of the same general form, namely <u>NP-be-NP</u>. In (46a) we must account for the fact that the reflexive pronoun is coreferential with an NP in the initial clause, while in (46b) the pronoun <u>him</u> cannot be coreferential with the previous NP. This is also the pattern found in non-clefted sentences:

(47) a. $Bill_i$ read a book about $himself_i$.

   b. *$Bill_i$ read a book about him_i.

This would then appear to be a case analogous to that

represented by the sentences of (8), i.e. one which would argue for a transformational derivation and against a base derivation.

Once again, however, sentences such as (45) (or (46)) do not, in fact, form counterexamples to the claim that pseudo-cleft sentences derive from a base source. The reason again is simply that as base-generated structures they do <u>not</u> form exceptions to otherwise general principles for assigning coreferentiality. This can be seen most easily by noting that the very same facts hold in copula sentences which are simple equational statements (i.e. which would not involve a clefting transformation):

(48) a. John$_i$'s favorite possession is a book about himself$_i$.

b. *John$_i$'s favorite possession is a book about him$_i$.

(49) John$_i$'s biggest worry is $\left\{ \begin{array}{l} \text{that} \\ \text{the} \end{array} \right\}$ photograph of

himself$_i$ which was taken last summer.

The facts of (48) are completely parallel with the facts of (46) and (47), but the sentences of (48) are only base-generated (i.e. do not undergo any clefting rule). (49) is also a simple basic equational statement, and there too the focus phrase contains an anaphoric expression which is co-referential with some item in the initial pre-copular phrase.

There are also examples in which the antecedent and the anaphoric expression are dominated by different $\underline{S}$ nodes:

(50) a. The greatest source of embarrassment that John$_i$

has to endure is $\begin{Bmatrix} \text{that} \\ \text{the} \end{Bmatrix}$ photograph of himself$_i$

which was taken last summer.

b. The most difficult project of all, which John$_i$ could hardly bring himself to complete, was the article about himself$_i$ that he was supposed to write for his publishers.

Sentences such as those of (50) are base-generated equative sentences, and yet they display the same sort of cross-copula coreferentiality patterns found in sentences such as (45) and (46).[14] Thus, if (45) and (46) are base-generated, they would not represent special cases for which the principles which determine coreferentiality would have to be extended in some ad hoc fashion. Sentences such as those of (48), (49), and (50) demonstrate that principles which determine coreferentiality relations will apply in copula sentences as well as non-copula sentences, and therefore sentences such as those of (45) and (46), if base-generated, cause no additional complication in the grammar.

To sum up briefly, we have pointed out that there are certain empirical claims inherent in the position that pseudo-cleft sentences have two distinct syntactic sources. In claiming that a certain subset of pseudo-cleft sentences are generated only by the base (e.g. pseudo-clefts with there within the initial clause and a definite NP in focus position), it should be the case that such sentences do not manifest the sort of grammatical connectedness which motivates a transformational derivation. We have examined a set of putative counterexamples, and we have found that they do not, in fact, represent cases of grammatical connectedness, in the sense intended. This is due to the fact that pseudo-cleft sentences of the form NP-be-NP behave like other copula sentences of that general form, and require no special principles to account for coreferentiality relations which hold across the copula.

If we now recall sentences such as those of (8), we can ask why it is that the coreferentiality patterns of those sentences in fact do constitute evidence for a transformational source. The crucial distinction between examples such as (8) and those such as (45) and (46) is that the focal phrases in (8) are verb phrases while those in (45) and (46) are noun phrases.

Consider an example with the form of (8):

(51) a. What John did was read a book about himself.

b. *What John thought Mary did was read a book
about himself.

A sentence such as (51a) cannot be generated by the base
expansion NP-be-NP, since the phrase read a book about himself
is a verb phrase, not an NP. Thus, to attempt to generate
such cases in the base would cause serious complications in
that an otherwise unnecessary base expansion would be
required (i.e. NP-be-VP); and, in addition, otherwise general
principles governing coreferentiality would have to be
extended in an ad hoc manner for just these cases.

On the other hand, sentences such as (45) and (46) have
quite a different status. That is, generating them in the
base does not entail constructing an otherwise unnecessary
base expansion, for the expansion NP-be-NP is required anyway
for simple equative statements. Further, as we have seen,
these particular sentences do not require any special grammatical principles beyond those independently required for
copula sentences in general. It should be the case, in
general, that pseudo-cleft sentences of the form NP-be-NP
do not display grammatical dependencies across the copula
of the sort which motivate a transformational analysis.[15]

We have attempted to make clear what sort of evidence
would argue against generating pseudo-cleft sentences in the
base. As far as I can determine, there are no examples which

indicate that generating pseudo-cleft sentences in this manner
results in loss of generality of the grammar. Specifically
with regard to certain cases involving existential there,
we have attempted to show that these are generated only in
the base.[16]

   We have seen that a dual source for pseudo-cleft sentences is not only unavoidable, but further, that there is
some positive syntactic evidence which indicates the need to
posit a source other than the transformational source. This
is to account for facts relating to There-Insertion. (In
the sections which follow, we will consider more evidence for
a dual source for pseudo-clefts.) We are therefore left with
a situation which can be described in the following sort of
diagram:

   (52)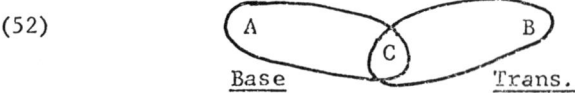

Pseudo-cleft sentences can derive from a source in the base,
or can be transformationally derived. Certain sentences,
(A), can be derived only in the base (e.g. There-Insertion).
Other pseudo-cleft sentences, (B), can only be transformationally derived (e.g. examples with reflexives). Finally,
a subset a pseudo-cleft sentences can derive from either
source. (We will show in Chapter 3 that for the subset of
pseudo-clefts which derive from either source, no systematic

semantic ambiguity can be associated with the derivational
ambiguity.) Having discussed why pseudo-cleft sentences
derive from both a transformational and a base source, we
should now consider the reasons for adopting the Extraction
Theory for pseudo-cleft sentences.[17]

6. Extraction or Deletion?

In the course of their discussion on pseudo-cleft sentences, Bach and Peters [1968] consider the Extraction Theory
proposed by Chomsky [1967], and attempt to show that such a
theory must be rejected. We will consider their criticisms
here, and attempt to show that they can be met. Further, we
will show that the Deletion Theory itself has serious defects
and that the Extraction Theory is in fact preferable.

The first objection raised by Bach and Peters concerns
the fact that on the Extraction Theory the focus of the
pseudo-cleft sentence cannot be determined at the deep
structure level. The predicate is empty at the deep level,
and there is no indication as to which particular constituent
of the embedded sentence will be extracted. The Extraction
Rule is stated as a general schema in order to express the

generalization that any major category can appear in focus
position. It is not until after the Extraction Rule has
applied that it is possible to determine the focus constituent
(in fact this is not possible until the level of phonetically
interpreted surface structure). We reject, of course,
notational tricks to achieve a marking of focus in deep
structure.

Notice, however, that in the Deletion Theory itself, the
focus position of the pseudo-cleft is occupied by a full sentence at the deep structure level (cf. (22)). The constituent
which ends up as the focus is that constituent which remains
after the deletion rule has applied. At the deep structure
level, before the application of the deletion rule, the focus
is not marked in any way. If one were to propose an interpretive rule to determine the focus at the deep structure
level, it would essentially have to be a restatement of the
deletion transformation. Such a rule would have to examine
both embedded sentences (e.g. S^2 and S^3 of (22)) and would
have to mark that portion of the rightmost sentence which is
not identical with any portion of the leftmost sentence as
the focus. This would therefore duplicate the operation of
the deletion transformation, and would needlessly complicate
the grammar. Thus, neither the Extraction nor Deletion
Theory provides a way to determine the focus constituent at

the deep structure level.

6.1. Evidence from Distribution of Pro-Forms. The second objection to the extraction theory which Bach and Peters advance involves certain problems concerning the distribution of pro-forms in the relative clauses of the pseudo-cleft. They note that _what_ is not usually used as a pro-form for animate nouns, as in:

(53) *What I persuaded to leave was Mary.

(54) *What is easy to please is John.

(It should be noted that their discussion is restricted to pseudo-cleft sentences with initial _what_-clauses.) However, it would not be strictly correct, as they point out, to restrict pseudo-cleft sentences with _what_ clauses such that only inanimate nouns may appear in focus position. Consider examples such as the following:

(55) What I saw was Mary. [18]

(56) *What I amazed was Mary.

(57) What concerned John was Mary.

(58) *What loves John is Mary.

The correct generalization, Bach and Peters maintain, is that the pattern of grammaticality of (55) - (58) is a function of the distributional pattern of the pro-form something:

(59) a. I saw something.

b. *I amazed something.

c. Something concerned John.

d. *Something loves John.

The sentences (55) - (58) constitute a problem for the Extraction Theory in the following way. When a constituent is operated on by the extraction rule, a representative pro-form is left in its place. For human nouns who is left behind, for inanimate nouns what is left behind, and so forth. Noting that (55) and (57) are grammatical, how is it that the pro-form what can be left in place of animate nouns? For example, (57) would derive from:

(60)

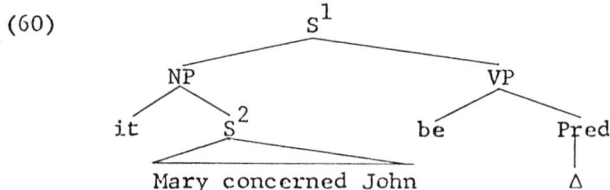

The extraction rule would have to move the constituent Mary into predicate position, leaving a pro-form behind. The pro-form could be what (as well as who for this particular case), and this specific characteristic would be expressed in the selectional restrictions of the verb concern. However, Bach and Peters point out (p. 6):

(61) "Now this is a decisive fact disconfirming all
Extracting Analyses in which the selection of the
pseudo-clefted noun phrase is carried out by a
transformation; for it is impossible to tell
at the time when this rule applies whether the
noun phrase selected could be replaced by something
since it can ... have been removed arbitrarily far
from the element(s) with which it participates in
selectional restrictions."

They go on to give examples such as the following:

(62) John is thought to have been amused by the joke.
If this were the embedded sentence within the pseudo-cleft
deep structure, there would be no way to tell, at the time
the extracting rule applied, whether or not the constituent
John could be replaced by what (i.e. (WH) something) as a
pro-form, since this constituent is removed from the elements
with which it enters into selectional restrictions. Therefore, the Extraction Theory fails to derive sentences such
as (55) and (57).

We will claim that such sentences are indeed not derived
by the Extraction Rule, but rather derive from the base.
Further, we will attempt to show that the basic source must
be the source for such sentences, and that the facts presented by Bach and Peters cause serious problems for the Deletion

Theory.

In this regard, consider the following situation. A verb such as <u>believe</u>, as Bach and Peters note, can take both <u>someone</u> and <u>something</u> as its object:

(63) a. I believe someone.

   b. I believe John.

(64) a. I believe something.

   b. I believe that John is intelligent.

Notice that while a pseudo-cleft such as (65a) is well-formed, (65b) is not:

(65) a. What I believe is that John is intelligent.

   b. *What I believe is John.

However, what is to block (65b) in the Deletion Theory, when deep structures such as the following are generated:

(66) [[the thing [I believe something]] be [I believe

    John]]

The first embedded sentence, <u>I believe something</u>, is well-formed, and so is the second sentence, <u>I believe John</u>. What prevents the deletion rule from applying, giving (65b)?

Bach and Peters attempt to solve this problem by noting that there are two distinct senses of the verb <u>believe</u> involved, and that for this reason the two occurrences of <u>believe</u> in (66) should be considered as non-identical verbs. To substantiate the claim that two verbs are involved, they

note, among other things, the possibility of the following
sort of contrast:

(67)   I believe the claim that John is a liar, but I

       believe him.

The two senses of the verb are quite clear, and it is perhaps
reasonable to consider the verbs of (66) as non-identical for
this reason.

This particular sort of explanation, however, fails for
other cases which are analogous. Consider, for example:

(68) a. *What he kicked was Mary.

     b. *What he found in the garden was Mary.

(69) a. What he kicked was the tree.

     b. What he found in the garden was the shovel.

The Deletion Theory predicts that sentences such as (68) are
well formed, since such sentences would derive from the
following sort of structure (for (68a)):

(70)

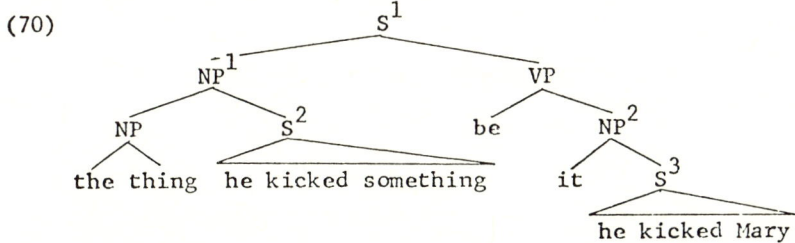

The verbs kick in S^2 and S^3 in (70) cannot be considered as
non-identical (i.e. the sense of the verb is completely independent of the marking for animacy of the object of the

verb). Nothing prevents the occurrence of he kicked in S^3 from being deleted. Completely analogous considerations hold for (68b).

The deviance of sentences such as (68a-b) resides in the fact that the semantic feature content of the NPs connected by the copula is in conflict (compare these with the analogous (28b)). It is not possible to equate an inanimate noun phrase (what he kicked, what he found) with an animate noun phrase (Mary). Such sentences are marked as deviant on the same basis as sentences such as (28b) and (30). (Therefore, they could not be generated in the base, since their semantic features do not agree in the relevant sense. They could not be generated by the Extraction Transformation either, since only the pro-form who is left behind for human NPs extracted.) However, the Deletion Theory generates sentences such as (68) from structures such as (70).

This observation uncovers a serious semantic problem with the deep structures posited by the Deletion Theory. It is reasonable to assume that sentences such as (28b), (30), and those of (68) are to be marked as deviant on the basis of a semantic principle of feature incompatibility (as discussed). But they cannot be ruled out (or marked as deviant) on that basis within the Deletion Theory, since the Deletion Theory as stated by Bach and Peters necessarily involves violation

of such feature agreement. Observe, once again, example (22).
The initial clause is a relative clause with the head noun
thing. In this case the head noun is marked as semantically
concrete. However, the noun phrase in focus position is an
NP which dominates a sentence, and is marked as semantically
abstract. Thus, a concrete NP is equated with an abstract
NP, and (22) should be as deviant as sentences such as:

    (71) a. *The car is John bought the car.

        b. *That chair is truth.

In order for the Deletion Theory to work, then, it is necessary
to abandon a principle of semantic feature agreement, and to
find an alternative explanation for the deviance of (28b),
(30), and (68).

    The problems we have been discussing are avoided entirely
if the Deletion Theory is abandoned in favor of the Extraction
Theory. That is, the Extraction Theory will not generate
sentences such as (68a) and (68b), because an animate NP has
been clefted in these cases and the Extraction Theory could
leave only the animate pro-form in place of the clefted NP
(i.e. who but not what). The question now arises as to how
sentences such as (55) and (57) are generated. These, notice,
could not be derived in the Extraction Theory since the inanimate pro-form what is found in clauses in which animate
NPs would have been extracted. Our claim is that there is no

problem connected with this, since sentences such as (55) and (57) will be generated by the base in any event, given the expansion NP-be-NP.

Consider as an example sentence (57). If this is generated in the base then we have a specificational statement in which the NP what concerned John is equated with the NP Mary. The reason why this is not ruled out is the following: the particular semantic properties of the verb concern (and verbs of this class), whatever these may be in detail, are such that inanimate pro-form subjects of such verbs (i.e. what, something, etc.) can be taken as referring to animates. For example, any theory must have a way to account for the following difference between verbs:

(72) a. Something concerns John, namely, Mary.

b. *Something kicked John, namely, Mary.

On the basis of examples such as (72) we conclude that it is a particular property of a given class of verbs whether or not inanimate pro-form subjects (or objects) of such verbs can be specified as animates. If this is true, then in a phrase such as what concerns John, the pro-form what will receive this specific semantic information projected by the verb concern. Thus, to equate what concerns John with Mary involves no semantic violations in (57), just as there are no violations in (72a).

On the other hand, in sentences such as (58) and (72b), there is indeed a semantic violation. The particular verbs _love_ and _kick_ do not allow inanimate subjects, and thus could not be generated. Furthermore, sentences such as (68a) and (68b) could not be generated, since the phrases <u>what he kicked</u> and <u>what he found in the garden</u> can only refer to inanimates, and thus cannot be equated with animates, such as <u>Mary</u>. The particular verbal expressions in these cases do not allow an inanimate pro-form object to refer to an animate entity. Thus, the base generates the correct set of cases, and excludes the deviant set, on the basis of semantic feature agreement.

Once again, we have a case analogous to the case involving existential <u>there</u>. That is, a certain class of pseudo-cleft sentences -- i.e., those with the pro-form <u>what</u> in the initial clause, but with animate NPs in focus position -- cannot be generated in either transformational theory discussed. Once again, the claim is that this set of pseudo-cleft sentences can be generated <u>only</u> in the base. If such sentences can be generated only in the base, then it should be true that factors which motivate a transformational analysis should not be found with such cases. Such sentences should not manifest the sort of grammatical connectedness which motivates a transformational analysis. A specific

counterexample to the position we have arrived at would be
one in which the form <u>what</u> appears in the initial clause,
where an animate NP is in focus position, yet where there is
grammatical connectedness across the copula which would
motivate a transformational analysis. This would be a case
which, if base generated, would cause otherwise unnecessary
complication in the grammar, or would constitute an exception
to otherwise general principles.

As far as I can determine, there are no such counterexamples. It should be borne in mind that sentences such as
the following:

(73) What concerns John is himself.

do not constitute counterexamples. Even though it appears as
if reflexivization operates "across the copula" in such cases,
it is not true that the coreferentiality patterns of sentences
such as (73) are parallel with patterns found in non-clefted
sentences (see note 3). Thus, consider, for example:

(74)
$$
\text{What John wants } \left\{ \begin{array}{c} \text{Bill} \\ \text{Mary} \end{array} \right\} \text{ to be concerned about}
$$
is himself.

In such sentences, the reflexive pronoun may be coreferential
either with <u>John</u> or <u>Bill</u>. In the non-clefted sentence,
however, there is only one possibility:

(75) John wants $\begin{Bmatrix} \text{Bill} \\ \text{*Mary} \end{Bmatrix}$ to be concerned about himself.

Hence, generating sentences such as (73) and (74) in the base
does not create otherwise unnecessary complication in the
grammar, since any theory must formulate rules for coreference
in cases where the reflexive pronoun forms the focus of the
sentence (i.e. bears the intonation center). Aside from such
cases as (73), there do not appear to be counterexamples of
the sort specified in the previous paragraph.

6.2. Arguments from the Derivation of Cleft Sentences.
We have argued in the previous section that the Deletion
Theory of pseudo-cleft sentences involves certain semantic
problems, i.e. it must be the case that semantically concrete
NPs can be equated with semantically abstract NPs. Furthermore, given this feature of the Deletion Theory, there is no
non-ad hoc means of excluding sentences such as (68a) and
(68b), since these can derive from structures such as (70).
So far, then, we have presented only negative evidence. At
this point, however, we will consider independent positive
evidence in favor of the Extraction Theory.

It is argued in Chapter 2 that cleft sentences derive

from pseudo-cleft sentences by a syntactic transformation which extraposes the initial clause of the pseudo-cleft to the end of the sentence, leaving the form __it__ in subject position. (For details of this derivation see Chapter 2). The Extraction Theory, but __not__ the Deletion Theory, allows us to derive certain cleft sentences which otherwise present serious problems for any analysis. We refer to cleft sentences which have prepositional phrases in focus position. Consider, for example:

(76) a. It was John who I gave the book to.

b. It was John to whom I gave the book.

c. It was to John that I gave the book.

If we search for pseudo-cleft sources for these sentences, we see that the first two sentences are not problematic, but the last, (76c), presents serious problems (pointed out in Akmajian [1970]). (76a) and (76b) can derive respectively from the following:

(77) (the one) who I gave the book to was John.

(78) (the one) to whom I gave the book was John.

However, what is the source for (76c)? We see that there is no well-formed pseudo-cleft source which gives us the proper form to derive (76c) (i.e. with a PP in focus position):

(79) a. *Who I gave the book was to John.

b. *Who I gave the book to was to John.

Given the Extraction Theory, however, this problem has
a natural solution. To see this, consider the following
input structure:

(80)

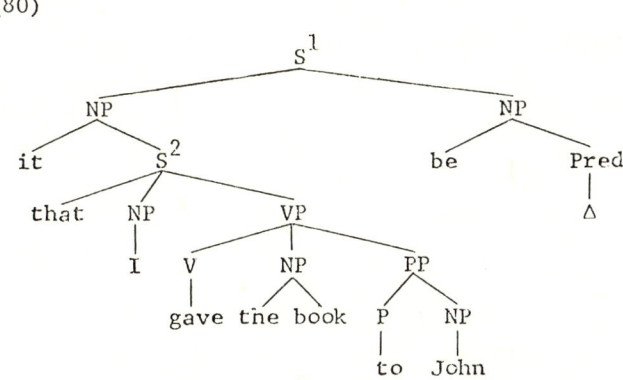

Let us consider various possibilities, given this input
structure. First of all, the extraction rule could extract
the NP John, leaving behind a pro-form (i.e. who):

(81)

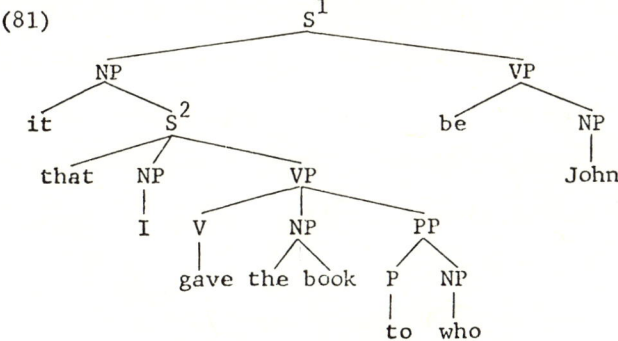

The WH-fronting rule can now move the WH word who to the
front of the sentence replacing that, thus deriving (77).

By extraposition of this initial clause we derive (76a).

Alternatively, the WH-fronting rule could transport the

entire PP dominating the WH-word, replacing the complementizer

that, deriving (78) and ultimately (76b). Consider now the

derivation of (76c). Given (80) as the input structure,

the extraction rule can operate to extract the PP and place

it in predicate position:

(82)

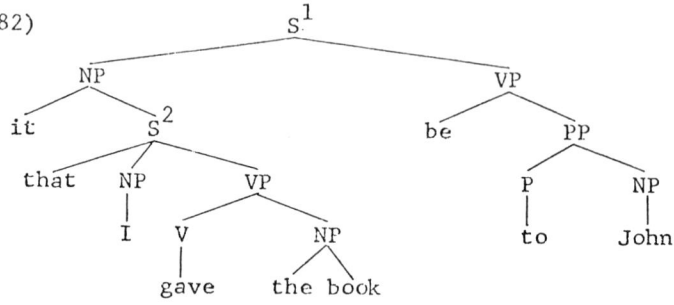

The crucial fact here is that the extraction rule leaves no

pro-form behind for the prepositional phrase. (This is

discussed further in the next chapter, where it is pointed

out that there are no syntactic pro-forms available in

English for PPs such as to John in (76c).) Since no pro-form

is left behind, there is no WH word to front, and this re-

sults in clauses headed by the complementizer that (i.e. that

is not lost by replacement with a WH-word). Structures such

as (82) then undergo extraposition to form cleft sentences.

(82), then, provides the source for (76c).

Notice, furthermore, that the extraction theory makes a crucial prediction for such cases: namely, that when the cleft has a PP such as <u>to John</u> in focus position, the following clauses <u>must</u> be headed by the complementizer <u>that</u>. Since no WH pro-form is left behind for PPs, only a <u>that</u> initial clause can result. This prediction is borne out:

(83) a. It was to John <u>that</u> I gave the book.

b. *It was to John who I gave the book.

c. *It was to John to whom I gave the book.

If we now examine the Deletion Theory with respect to this data, we see that the Deletion Theory provides no account for sentences such as (76c). The closest deep structure source for (76c) would have to be:

(84)

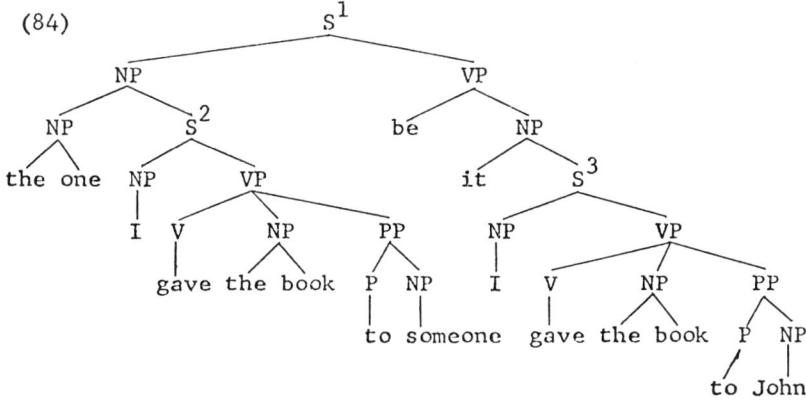

The deletion rule could apply to derive sentences (77) and (78), and these present no problems. However, (76c) could not be derived. First of all, the preposition in S^3 would always be deleted, since it is identical with the preposition in S^2, and therefore we could not derive the prepositional phrase in focus position. Furthermore, even if we grant that by some means we could derive the PP in focus position, we would still be left with the problem of how to get rid of the preposition in the initial clause:

(85) a. *The one who I gave the book to was to John.

b. *The one to whom I gave the book was to John.

The Deletion Theory, then, involves at least two problems: (a) how to avoid deletion of the preposition in focus position, and (b) how to eliminate the preposition in the initial clause. Furthermore, in the Deletion Theory there would appear to be no reason at all why cleft sentences with PPs such as to John in focus position must have that clauses.

7. The Embedded Question Alternative

Before ending our discussion of the syntactic derivation of pseudo-cleft sentences, we should consider a modification of the Deletion Theory which has been suggested recently

(in unpublished papers by E. Clifton [1969], R. Faraci [1970],
as well as J.R. Ross [personal communication]). The suggestion
advanced is to modify the Deletion Theory so that the initial
clause of the pseudo-cleft has the status of an embedded
question, rather than the status of a relative clause. Thus,
for a sentence such as (16a) (repeated here as (86a)) the
underlying structure on this proposal would roughly be (86b):

(86) a. What John read was a book about himself.

b.

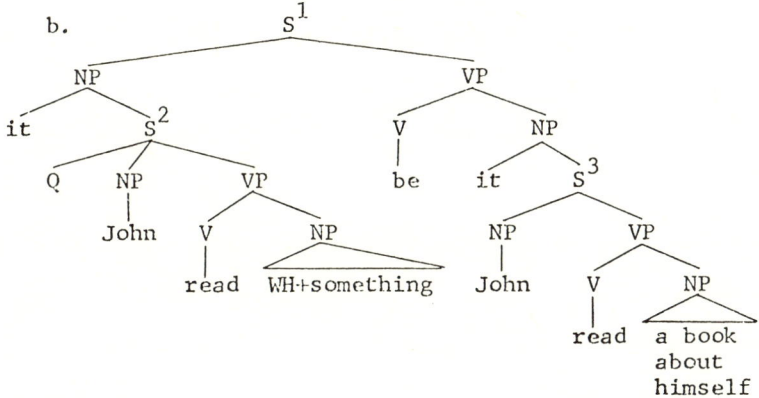

The Deletion Rule would apply to such a structure, as
before. [19]

The proposed change saves the Deletion Theory from the
semantic problems mentioned earlier. That is, if the initial
clause is a question rather than a relative clause, as in (22),
then it will have the status of a semantically abstract clause,
and the NP dominating the question will be semantically an
abstract NP. Thus, both the initial and final clauses of the

pseudo-cleft deep structure will always be abstract, and
therefore the problem of conflicting feature composition will
vanish, and the objections raised in section 6.1 no longer
hold. However, we will show in this section that this proposed modification is incorrect for several reasons, and
must be rejected. Furthermore, while this approach solves
certain semantic problems, we will show that it leads to other
equally serious semantic problems.[20]

First let us note that the proposed hypothesis (hence-
forth the Question Theory) has some initial plausibility.
That is, the first clause of the pseudo-cleft acts as a
question (and is often an echo of a question which is being
answered) in that it contains a variable, and the focus of
the pseudo-cleft acts as an answer to the initial question in
that it provides a specification of the variable. This is not
reason enough to generate the initial clause as a question,
but does indicate that the proposal reflects a certain
intuition about the use of pseudo-cleft sentences.[21]

The most interesting arguments for this proposal are
advanced by Faraci [1970], the central argument of which has
to do with the fact that embedded questions, but not free
relatives, may appear in clefted form.[22] Consider, for
example:

(87) a. What it was that John bought was not clear.

     b. *I threw out what it was that John bought.

Noting this fact, Faraci goes on to point out that (at least
in his speech) the initial clause of the pseudo-cleft may be
in clefted form:

(88) What it was that John bought was a car.

Thus, the argument is that just as the embedded question, (87a),
can be in clefted form, so can the initial clause of the
pseudo-cleft, (88). However, the free relative in (87b) may
not be in clefted form. (It should be noted here, however,
that for my own speech sentences such as (88) are more or less
marginal.)

Faraci goes on to point out additional, but weaker,
evidence in favor of the question hypothesis. For example,
he maintains that the distribution of certain adverbs is
identical in embedded questions and pseudo-clefts, but
different in free relatives. Thus, compare the following:

(89) a. What, exactly, John bought is not clear.

     b. *I threw out what, exactly, John bought.

     c. What, exactly, John bought was a car.

(Again we give these sentences in terms of Faraci's judgements.) The argument here is that the adverb exactly can
appear in the embedded question (89a) as well as the pseudo-
cleft (89c), but not in the free relative. Therefore, the

initial clause of the pseudo-cleft is not a free relative,
but an embedded question. (Once again, however, for my own
speech (89c) is ungrammatical.) We must now show, however,
that even though there is some initial plausibility for the
hypothesis, there is quite a bit of evidence against the
proposal.[23]

The first set of arguments which we present indicates
that the initial clause of the pseudo-cleft cannot be an
embedded question, since we do not find certain morphemes or
formal properties which we expect to find in embedded questions. For example, if the initial clause were an embedded
question, we would expect to find else and ever, but we do
not. Consider:

    (90) a. What else he bought is not clear.

        b. What he ever worked on is simply not known.

    (91) a. *What else he bought was a car.

        b. *What he ever worked on was his thesis.

We see that the embedded questions of (90) admit else and
ever; however, the clauses of the pseudo-cleft in (91) do
not. Pursuing this line further, we note that if the clause
of the pseudo-cleft were a question we would expect to find
whether-clauses, which-clauses, and clauses with double
occurrences of WH words. Compare the embedded questions of
(92) with the pseudo-cleft sentences of (93):

(92) a. Whether he will go is not known at this time.

b. Which book he read is hard to determine.

c. Who kissed whom is not clear.

(93) a. *Whether he will go is yes.[24]

b. *Which book he read was War and Peace.

c. *Who kissed whom was John kissed Mary.

Comparison of (92) and (93) reveals that the initial clause of the pseudo-cleft in fact does not behave like an embedded question. Further counter-evidence is found in the distribution of any in embedded questions. Since any is found in embedded questions we should also get it in pseudo-clefts in the initial clause, but we do not:

(94) a. I don't know what makes any sense.

b. *What makes any sense is not John's theory.

Faraci attempts to counter this by claiming that initial embedded questions with any are ungrammatical in general. However, examples such as the following show that this is not true:

(95) What anyone can do about the war now is unclear.

As a final argument of this sort, note that in embedded questions it is possible to have a preposed prepositional phrase; however, in the clause of the pseudo-cleft this is impossible:

(96) a. To whom one should give the application form

is not clear.

b. *To whom one should give the application form

is the registrar.

Thus, the Question Theory makes false predictions as to the
possible form of pseudo-cleft sentences.

However, there are more serious defects. If the Question
Theory is correct, then pseudo-cleft sentences with headless
initial clauses are completely unrelated to pseudo-clefts
with initial relative clauses, such as:

(97) The thing that John wants is a car.

In (97) the initial clause is a genuine relative, a fact which
can be tested by noting that it is impossible for the clause
to occur in cleft form:

(98) *The thing that it is that John wants is a car.

Since the clause of (97) is a relative clause, it should bear
no relation to the sentence:

(99) What John wants is a car.

since the initial clause here is supposedly a question.

In order to preserve the relation between sentences such
as (99) and (97), Faraci proposes to derive sentences such as
(97) from sentences such as (99), in the manner of the
derivation of concealed questions proposed by Baker [1968].
Baker proposes to derive sentences such as (100a) from (100b):

(100) a. I finally found out the brand she uses.

   b. I finally found out which brand she uses.

In a similar manner, Faraci wishes to derive the thing that John wants from what John wants, thus claiming that the former clause is really a question. However, if this were the case we would expect sentences such as (98), since questions may occur in clefted form.[25] Therefore, the Embedded Question Theory forces us to treat (97) and (99) as unrelated. One would expect some difference if in fact the clause of one were a question and that of the other a relative, but (97) and (99) are synonymous in this case.

We present now evidence that the Question Theory must face serious semantic problems connected with the referentiality of noun phrases. Consider an example such as:

(101) What John ate was the steak.

The nominal phrases underlined in (101) are both understood to be referential, i.e. to have a specific referent in the universe of discourse. Now if this is the case, then the phrase what John ate cannot be an embedded question, since embedded questions cannot be used to refer to objects in the world, and do not have specific referents in the sense that relative nominals do.

We can in fact test the claim that phrases such as what John ate are referential NPs in several ways. Consider first the fact that in a specificational statement, the post-copular NP and the pre-copular NP must both be referential. This is shown by comparing sentences such as the following:

(102) a. The thing that John ate was the steak.

b. *Some thing that John ate was the steak.

Thus, a phrase such as some thing that John ate, which is understood to be non-referential, i.e. to have no specific referent in the universe of discourse, cannot occur in a specificational statement where the post-copular NP is referential. (This, we should note, is completely parallel with the property mentioned earlier that in specificational statements relevant semantic features must agree.[26]) Returning now to (101) we note that since the post-copular NP is referential, the initial nominal must also be referential. Hence, it cannot be an embedded question.

Another simple test for the claim that the initial clause of the pseudo-cleft must be referential has to do with the fact that appositive relative clauses can be adjoined to such phrases. Appositive clauses can be adjoined only to NPs which have specific referents, as we see from the following examples:

(103) a. The man, who was very tall, addressed us.

b. *Some man, who was very tall, addressed us.

Given this fact, we now note that such appositives can be

adjoined to the initial clauses of pseudo-cleft sentences, but not to embedded questions:

(104)   What John got from his father yesterday, which was very expensive, was that Jaguar XKE.[27]

(105)   a.   *No one knows what John got from his father yesterday, which was quite expensive.

b.   *What John got from his father yesterday, which was quite expensive, is a mystery.[28]

The embedded questions of (105) cannot take appositive relatives, since such clauses are not referential.

Returning for a moment to sentences such as (87) and (88), we should note that Faraci's evidence from clefting possibilities is weaked a great deal by the fact that certain relative clauses can in fact occur in clefted form. These are, in particular, relative clauses with whatever:

(106)   a. Whatever it was that John bought cost him a lot of money.

b. She threw away whatever it was that John bought.

The phrases with whatever are clearly not questions. Therefore, even if sentences such as (88) exist, they do not show that the clause of the pseudo-cleft must be an embedded question, since we see here that certain relative clauses can occur in clefted form.

What seems to be the relevant generalization here is that

non-referential clauses may occur in clefted form. This
generalization covers embedded questions, which we have seen
are not referential, and also clauses with whatever, since
these, too, are non-referential. This can be seen simply in
the fact that such clauses cannot occur in pseudo-cleft sentences, nor can appositive relatives be adjoined to them:

(107) a. *Whatever (it was that) John bought was a car.

b. *Whatever John bought, which cost a lot, was
broken two days later.

Therefore, we claim that non-referential clauses occur in
clefted form. (If this is the case, it shows why, for the
speech of certain speakers, including myself, sentences such
as (88) are judged as deviant. That is, it is not possible
for the initial clause to be non-referential if the final
clause is referential.)

8. Summary

The objective of this chapter has been to establish the
basic hypothesis that pseudo-cleft sentences can derive from
two syntactic sources within the grammar. This is the case
since for one class of pseudo-cleft sentences, a

transformational analysis is necessary, and for another class
a base source is necessary. Furthermore, there is no non-
ad hoc way to prevent the base from generating pseudo-cleft
sentences in any event. While given classes of pseudo-cleft
sentences derive either from one source or the other, there
is partial overlap, and for a subset of pseudo-cleft
sentences, either source is possible. We have attempted to
show that of the current transformational theories of pseudo-
cleft sentences, the Extraction Theory must be chosen, given
that the Deletion Theory (and its variant, the Question
Theory) gives rise to various semantic and syntactic problems
which are not found with the Extraction Theory.

FOOTNOTES TO CHAPTER 1

1. Many speakers find sentences such as (2a) unacceptable
   (or less acceptable than sentences (2b)-(2f)) but judge
   as acceptable sentences (2b)-(2f). For this particular
   dialect we can assume that sentences such as (2a) obligatorily become cleft sentences (e.g. "It was Agnew who
   Nixon chose"). Note that correlated with the fact that
   (2a) is unacceptable is the fact that in cleft sentences
   the only WH clauses which can appear in extraposed
   position are who clauses (cf. *"It was a car what I
   bought"). For further discussion, see Chapter 2.

2. We assume, of course, that the sentences of (3) have the
   same foci as the sentences of (1) and (2). For example,
   sentence (3) is a paraphrase of sentences (1a) and (2a) if
   the intonation center of (3) comes on the constituent
   Agnew:

(2) (cont'd.)

    (i) a. The one Nixon chose was Agnew.

       b. Who Nixon chose was Agnew.

       c. Nixon chose Agnew.

The sentences of (i) all have identical foci and pre-suppositions (i.e. focus on _Agnew_, with the presupposition that Nixon chose someone). Thus, clefted and non-clefted sentences are paraphrases provided the focus constituents are identical.

3. It should be noted that Bach and Peters use certain examples involving reflexives which do not, in fact, motivate a transformational analysis. An example of this sort given by them is:

    (i) What the missile damaged was itself.

Notice that this is a case in which the reflexive pronoun is the sole item in focus position, and bears the intonation center of the sentence. In cases such as this one, in which the reflexive is the focus, the restrictions governing coreferentiality of reflexive pronouns are relaxed, i.e. pseudo-cleft sentences of this form are not parallel with non-clefted sentences. Consider:

    (ii) a. The one John wants Mary to describe
          is himself.

(3) (cont'd.)

        b. The one John claimed had been cheated

           was himself.

Note that there are no non-clefted sentences parallel with these:

      (iii) a. *John wants Mary to describe himself.

           b. *John claimed that himself had been

              cheated.

Thus, pseudo-cleft sentences with reflexives as the sole focus do not provide motivation for deep structures in which the phrase marker for the corresponding non-clefted sentence appears. (For further discussion of this phenomenon, see Chapter 4, note 1.)

In contrast, notice the sentences of (8). In these cases the reflexive pronoun is part of a larger phrase, and, in particular does not bear the intonation center. In such cases where the reflexive pronoun is within the focus phrase but does not constitute the sole focus, the coreferentiality patterns in clefted and non-clefted sentences are then parallel. It is this parallelism which motivates a transformational analysis. It is interesting to note, once again, that even in sentences such as (8), if the reflexive is given the highest stress, then the coreferentiality patterns change:

(3) (cont'd.)

> (iv) What John wants Mary to do is wash HIMSELF.
>
> (cf. (8b)). Thus, when using coreferentiality patterns as examples of grammatical connectedness in pseudo-cleft sentences, one must be careful to choose examples in which the anaphoric expression within the focus phrase does not bear the highest stress, either optionally or obligatorily.

4. For example, if pseudo-cleft sentences were to be generated only in the base, in essentially their surface form, then there would be complication in generating derived phrases such as easy to please and eager to please, for reasons which have now become well known. See Chomsky [1965].

5. It should be added that there are further arguments from grammatical connectedness which have been discussed. For example, J.R. Ross [class lectures] has pointed out the parallelism of clefted and non-clefted sentences with respect to the distribution of some/any. Consider, for example:

> (i) a. I doubt that $\left\{ \begin{array}{c} \text{anyone} \\ \text{*someone} \end{array} \right\}$ needs this money.

(5) (cont'd.)

    b. I don't doubt that $\left\{\begin{array}{l}{}^{*}\text{anyone}\\ \text{someone}\end{array}\right\}$ needs this money.

  (ii) a. What I doubt is that $\left\{\begin{array}{l}\text{anyone}\\ {}^{*}\text{someone}\end{array}\right\}$ needs

    this money.

    b. What I don't doubt is that $\left\{\begin{array}{l}{}^{*}\text{anyone}\\ \text{someone}\end{array}\right\}$ needs

    this money.

Once again, the facts manifested in the pseudo-cleft sentence are parallel with those manifested in the non-clefted sentence. Pairs such as (i) and (ii) provide additional support for deriving pseudo-cleft sentences from deep structure sources which incorporate the phrase markers for the corresponding non-clefted sentences.

6. We modify Chomsky's theory somewhat, however, by stipulating that the extraction rule leaves behind a pro-form with the marking [+WH], and we drop Chomsky's rule which converts it+that to what.

7. The semantic interpretation of such deep structures as (17) is discussed in Chapter 3, section 4.1., where it is pointed out that the empty predicate in such structures

(7) (cont'd.)

causes no semantic complications.

8. We should note that it is just this base expansion that is
required by the deletion theory to form the deep structure
of the pseudo-cleft (cf. (22)). Further, this expansion
is required by the Extraction Theory whenever the focus of
the pseudo-cleft is an NP. Recall that the term PRED is
used as a cover term for the nodes which can appear after
the copula. Thus, (17) is more accurately represented as:

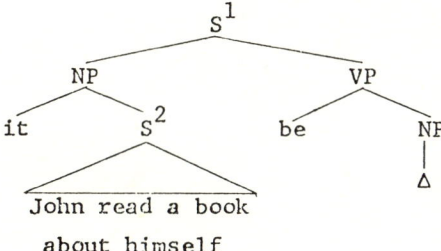

This tree, we note, requires the base expansion
[NP - be - NP].

9. For clarification of the term 'specificational statement'
see Chapter 3, section 2.1.

10. Note that it would be too strong to state that the NPs
being equated must be identical with respect to the

(10) (cont'd.)

features which play a role in selectional restrictions.
Consider, for example:

(i) That person over there is the man I know.

Thus, the NP person is neutral with regard to the marking
for the semantic feature (Male), but (i) is still well-
formed. The crucial distinction between (i) and (31) is
that in (i) the two NPs connected by the copula do not
have distinct markings for the feature (i.e. (-) vs. (+)).
In what follows we will speak of feature 'agreement';
however, the term 'agreement' will be used to mean
"identity or non-distinctness".

11. It is not clear that the rule can in fact apply in such an
environment, given the oddity of sentences such as:

(i) ?The thing that there was in the car was my hat.

(ii) ?I threw away the thing that there was in the car.

This seems to be related to the fact that relative clauses
cannot occur in clefted form:

(iii) *The thing that it was that was in the car
was my hat.

(Such sentences are discussed further in section 7.) That
is, it is impossible to relativize an item from post-
copular position in bound relatives. Note, however, that

(11) (cont'd.)

this is possible in free relatives:

(iv) I threw out what there was in the car.

12. It should be kept in mind that sentences such as the following:

(i) What there was in the car was a hat.
could derive from either the transformational or the base source. Since There-Insertion operates on indefinite NPs, a sentence such as (i) could be derived from a structure such as (36). It could, of course, also be generated in the base, with the expansion NP-be-NP.

13. Incidentally, note further that for (43) there is no corresponding non-clefted sentence, with or without existential there. In particular, the following are not possible:

(i) *His own pistol was next to Bill.

(ii) *There was his own pistol next to Bill.

In neither case is the reflexive possessive coreferential with the NP Bill. Yet, if it were argued that (43) were derived transformationally, such a derivation would indeed require (ii). Since neither (i) nor (ii) is possible, this provides further support for the view that sentences

(13) (cont'd.)

such as (43) are generated only in the base.

14. Note, in particular, that sentences such as (50) are not
pseudo-cleft sentences, nor could they undergo a clefting
transformation. They would not be labeled as pseudo-
cleft sentences since the heads of the initial phrases
of the sentences of (50) are not semantic variables, in
the sense discussed in regard to the sentences of (1) and
(2). Further, these cannot undergo a clefting transformation for the reason that there is no place within the
pre-copular phrase from which the post-copular phrase
could originate. For example, the basic equation of
(50b) is:

    (i) <u>The most difficult project of all</u> was

        <u>the article about himself that he was supposed</u>

        <u>to write for his publishers.</u>

The reason why (i) could not undergo any sort of clefting
transformation is that there is simply no place in the
initial phrase from which the post-copular phrase could
be extracted. Rather, (i) (and the sentences of (48),
(49), and (50)) are simple basic equations. Such examples
can be multiplied indefinitely. Consider:

(14) (cont'd.)

    (ii) a. The only mystery John$_i$ can't solve is

$$\left\{\begin{array}{l}\text{that}\\\text{the}\end{array}\right\}$$ article about himself$_i$ which appeared

in _Playboy_.

    b. The cross that John$_i$ has to bear is the article about himself$_i$ which exposes all those embarrassing details.

Again, these are basic equational statements, in which there is no way for the post-copular phrase to originate within the initial phrase.

15. In other words, it turns out that pseudo-cleft sentences which display a syntactic form other than the form NP-be-NP are those sentences which provide motivation for a transformational analysis. For example, these would include pseudo-cleft sentences with VPs and Adjective Phrases in focus position (cf. "What she did was wash herself vigorously", "What John is is easy to please"). Further, as we discuss in section 6.2. and in Chapter 2, pseudo-cleft sentences with PPs in focus position also motivate a transformational analysis (in particular, these form the basis for cleft sentences; cf. "It was to John that I gave the book"). Our claim is that sentences of

(15) (cont'd.)

the form NP-be-NP do not provide support for a transformational analysis. (Needless to say, this claim is obviously based on the assumption that phrases such as wash herself, easy to please, and to John are not noun phrases.)

16. The argument that sentences such as (34) can only derive from the base source depends crucially on the existence of a restriction prohibiting There-Insertion from operating on definite NPs. Kenneth Hale has suggested to me a way in which this argument might be answered. That is, Hale points out that one might claim that There-Insertion is not restricted only to indefinite NPs, and that sentences such as (35) should be generated as well-formed but subject to a special semantic interpretation (not associated with cases which have indefinite NPs). Specifically, it has often been noted that existential there can co-occur with syntactically definite NPs whenever there is a sense of "listing" involved. For example:

> (i) What did you find in the car?
>
> (ii) Well, there was the picnic basket, the blanket, the inner tube, the broom you got for Christmas, and a photo of Spiro Agnew.

(16) (cont'd.)

Hale thus suggests that one might argue that sentences
such as:

(iii)   There was $\left\{ \begin{array}{l} \text{the jack you gave me} \\ \text{my hat} \end{array} \right\}$ in the car.

should be generated as well-formed, and subject to the
special interpretation of "listing", as with (ii).   If
(iii) were allowed in this manner, then in a structure
such as (36) There-Insertion could apply in S^2, thereby
deriving sentences such as (34) from the transformational
(extraction) source.   (Notice, incidentally, that this
would be possible only with the Extraction Theory -- the
arguments against the Deletion Theory would still hold
in any event.   That is, whether or not There-Insertion
were formulated to apply on definite NPs, the point is
that the rule of There-Insertion would still destroy the
identity conditions required by the Deletion Theory.)

It seems to me that such an approach would be mistaken.   That is, as for my own judgements, sentences such
as (iii) are not acceptable, even with some special interpretation of "listing".   I would not judge sentence (iii)
as an appropriate answer to (i): the sense of "listing"
arises only when there is in fact a list of more than one
item given, and the longer the list the more acceptable

(16) (cont'd.)

the sentence (obviously, within reasonable limits).
Thus, consider:

    (iv) What did you find in the car?

    (v) a. *There was the jack you gave me in the car.

        b. ?There was the jack you gave me and the lug wrench in the car.

        c. There was the jack you gave me, the lug wrench, the radio, and the picnic basket in the car.

Furthermore, at least for my own speech, sentences such as (34) do not carry a sense of "listing", but are interpreted just as sentences with indefinite NPs are. Compare, for example:

    (vi) a. What there was in the car was my hat.

        b. What there was in the car was a hat.

These are both interpreted in the same way -- the case with the definite NP has no special interpretation.

The claim that There-Insertion may operate with definite NPs has certain consequences which are more serious, however. Once the restrictions on There-Insertion are relaxed in this manner, we are then left with no explanation for the following facts:

(16) (cont'd.)

   (vii) a. If you're looking for your coat, there's

          one in the bedroom.

       b. *If you're looking for your coat, there's

          it in the bedroom.

Sentences such as (vii-b) are direct counterexamples to

the claim that There-Insertion may operate with definite

noun phrases. (As far as I know, there are no speakers

who accept such sentences.)

   Similar examples have been discussed in a recent

squib by Joan Bresnan [1970]. In discussing pronominali-

zation, Bresnan argues that (viii-a) cannot derive from

(viii-b):

   (viii) a. Some students think that they are running

             the show.

        b. Some students$_i$ think that some students$_i$ are

           running the show.

If (viii-b) were the underlying form for (viii-a), it

should be possible for There-Insertion to apply on the

embedded sentence, producing:

   (ix) Some students$_i$ think that there are some

         students$_i$ running the show.

It should then be possible for pronominalization to apply

on the upper cycle, producing:

(x)   *Some students$_i$ think that there are they

running the show.

Bresnan argues, however, that sentences such as (x)
cannot be generated if the pronoun <u>they</u> appears in the
underlying form (i.e. (viii-a) would form the underlying
form, as such). There-Insertion cannot apply when there
is a definite pronoun present, and hence (viii-a) could
not become (x). If the restrictions on There-Insertion
are relaxed so that the rule may apply with definite NPs,
then there is no way to block sentence (x) above. If the
rule is restricted to applying with indefinites, then
there is an explanation for sentences such as (x).

As for sentences such as (v-c), these are permissible
only under special circumstances, and it is not clear how
these are generated. Note further that, at least in my
own speech, such sentences occur in restricted environments. In particular, they cannot be questioned or
negated:

(xi) a. *Was there the jack, the lug wrench, and the

picnic basket in the car?

b. cf: Was there a jack, a lug wrench, and a

picnic basket in the car?

(16) (cont'd.)

    (xii) a. *There wasn't the jack, the lug wrench, and
the picnic basket in the car.

        b. cf: There wasn't a jack, a lug wrench, and
a picnic basket in the car.

In any event, however sentences such as (v-c) are to be
generated, it would be wrong to assume that sentences
such as (v-a) could be generated in the same way, for
reasons given above.

17. The arguments for a transformational source for pseudo-
clefts which have been presented so far are independent
of any particular transformational theory of pseudo-
clefts. Thus, the existence of a dual source for
pseudo-clefts is an issue which is independent of the
issue of the choice of a particular transformational
theory of pseudo-clefts.

18. I do not find sentences such as (55) as acceptable as
sentences such as (57). The reason has to do with the
fact that the pro-form what most naturally functions to
refer to human nouns with verbs which take as subjects
(or objects) both abstract nouns and human nouns. For
example:

(18) (cont'd.)

  (i) a. The lack of justice concerned John.

   b. Mary's situation concerned John.

   c. Mary concerned John.

In a certain sense the NP <u>Mary</u> in (i-c) is abstract in that particular context. Thus, the pre-form <u>what</u> is appropriate. (I am grateful to Morris Halle for pointing out these facts.)

19. Since this modification of the Deletion Theory still retains the basic deletion process, it is also subject to the criticisms advanced in the previous section (i.e. there is still no natural way to derive prepositional phrases in focus position).

20. One of the problems faced by this theory is that while the pseudo-cleft necessarily derives from a deep structure which has the interpretation of an equation of two <u>abstract</u> NPs, the surface structures which derive from these may not have the same interpretation. Consider:

  (i) a. What he cooked was that steak.

   b. [[Q-he-cooked-what] be

    [he-cooked-that-steak]]

A sentence such as (i-a) derives from a structure such as

(20) (cont'd.)

(i-b). (i-b) is an equation of two abstract NPs, but (i-a) does not have this interpretation since the NP <u>that steak</u> is semantically concrete. Therefore, the semantic reading of the deep structure (i-b) is not preserved by the Deletion Rule.

21. J.R. Ross [personal communication] has suggested that the deep structure of the pseudo-cleft, on the Embedded Question Theory, should actually be (roughly) the following:

(i) [[The answer to the question (of)

[Q-John-read-what]] is

[John-read-a book about himself]]

However, it seems to me that it would be difficult to motivate the presence of the lexical items <u>answer</u> and <u>question</u>, and it is hard to see what syntactic function these items would fulfill. At any rate, this suggestion (as well as Faraci's) is subject to the criticisms we advance in this section.

22. For a discussion of the differences between free relatives and embedded questions, see Baker [1970].

23. Further, it is necessary to point out that the parallels
    between pseudo-cleft sentences and question-answer pairs
    can be accounted for in other ways. In Chapter 3 we
    present a system of semantic notation which can be used in
    simple ways to capture the similarities between questions,
    answers, and pseudo-cleft sentences.

24. (93a) is particularly damaging to Ross' suggestion, since
    the following is well-formed:

    (i) The answer to the question of whether he will
         go is yes.

    From this well-formed deep structure, however, no well-
    formed pseudo-cleft can be derived. (Some of these
    counterexamples, by the way, are also noted by Faraci.)

25. Faraci in fact maintains that sentences such as (98) are
    well-formed for him, and these constitute evidence for him
    that the clauses of such sentences are in fact questions.
    Such sentences are ungrammatical for myself and others I
    have checked, however.

26. Thus far we have stated this agreement phenomenon in terms
    of agreement of semantic features which play a role in

(26) (cont'd.)

selectional restrictions. It is not clear to me whether
the property of referentiality is also a semantic feature
in this sense. In any event, this property must be a
property of both NPs of a specificational statement.

27. Sentences such as (104) provide additional evidence against
the specific proposal mentioned in note 21. That is, the
following is impossible:

   (i)   *The answer to the question of what John got
         from his father, which was very expensive,
         was a Jaguar XKE.

28. The examples in (105) do not depend crucially on the
presence of negation (cf. (105a). For example, consider:

   (i)   *We all realize what John got from his father,
         which was very expensive.

Notice, furthermore, that various sorts of parenthetical
clauses can occur with the initial clauses of pseudo-cleft
sentences, but not with embedded questions. Consider:

   (ii) a. What he cooked for us -- the tastiest dish
           I've had this week -- was an English mutton
           pie.

(28) (cont'd.)

    b. What he saw in the box -- a sight which

       terrified him -- was a dismembered hand.

Compare these with the following:

    (iii) a. *What he cooked for us -- the tastiest dish

        I've had this week -- was obvious to all of us.

       b. *We do not know what he saw in the box -- a

        sight that terrified him.

These facts indicate, again, that embedded questions and

the WH clauses of pseudo-clefts do not behave alike.

CHAPTER 2

THE SYNTACTIC DERIVATION OF CLEFT SENTENCES

1. Deriving Cleft Sentences from Pseudo-Cleft Sentences

There is a great deal of similarity between pseudo-cleft sentences and their corresponding cleft sentences. If we examine as an example a pair of sentences such as:

(1) a. (The one) who Nixon chose was Agnew

    b. It was Agnew who Nixon chose

we note that the pseudo-cleft and its corresponding cleft sentence express the same grammatical relations, share the same presuppositions, have the same focus, in short, they are synonymous and are used interchangeably. Since the semantic representation of pseudo-cleft and corresponding cleft sentences is identical, we will discuss the semantic representation of both syntactic forms in Chapter 3. The objective of this chapter, however, is to provide a general account of the syntactic derivation of cleft sentences, and in particular, to show that cleft sentences derive syntactically from pseudo-cleft sentences.

We will propose specifically that cleft sentences are derived from pseudo-cleft sentences by a transformation which
extraposes the initial clause of the pseudo-cleft to the end
of the sentence. We refer to this rule as the Cleft Extraposition rule, and its operation can be illustrated by the
following pair of phrase markers:

(2) a.

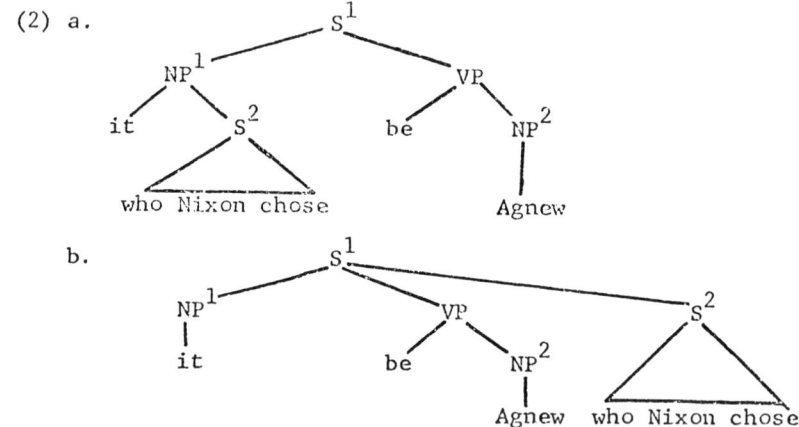

Note here that the initial clause of the pseudo-cleft is a
free relative, not a bound relative, and we show in a later
section that the cleft source (2a) must ultimately derive from
a deep structure with an empty predicate such as that posited
in the Extraction Theory. For the bulk of the discussion,
however, it does not matter whether the initial clause is
thought of as a free or bound relative, since both kinds of
relative clause share certain properties which are crucial for

the derivation of cleft sentences.[1]

2. On Motivating Transformational Rules

Whenever a new transformational rule is proposed, it is of course necessary to provide ample justification for the particular transformational derivation advanced. The question arises, however, as to what sort of justification -- i.e. what kind of evidence -- is required to establish a given analysis. In particular, we refer here to the tendency in recent work to justify transformational analyses on the basis of semantic considerations. We have noted, for example, that pseudo-cleft sentences and their corresponding cleft sentences are synonymous, and it is easy to see that semantic violations (e.g. selectional violations) in one would also be matched in the other. However, arguments from similarity of selectional restrictions and grammatical relations should be secondary in attempting to justify a transformational analysis.

It is imperative to provide independent <u>syntactic</u> evidence for proposed analyses, where by the term 'syntactic' we mean the strictly <u>formal</u> properties of given constructions.

What we wish to bring out here is that the analysis proposed
here for cleft sentences is not justified on the basis of
semantic considerations, but rather, the arguments which will
be given are all arguments from syntactic form of the cleft
construction. The analysis is justified primarily on the
basis of the fact that one can predict complicated syntactic
agreement patterns by deriving cleft sentences from pseudo-
cleft sentences. Further, we would claim that any transformational analysis proposed must be justified by formal evidence of this sort. With this in mind, we turn now to the
specific evidence for the proposal.

3. Evidence for the Proposal

3.1. Evidence from Verb Agreement Patterns.
One of the
most interesting syntactic properties of cleft sentences is
the verbal agreement pattern. I will be concerned primarily
with my own dialect, which I label Dialect I, however, I will
discuss two other dialects as well. In Dialect I, (which is
the dialect of most speakers I have interviewed) the following is the typical pattern:

(3) a. It's me who <u>is</u> responsible.

b. It's you who <u>is</u> responsible.

c. It's him who <u>is</u> responsible.

d. It's $\begin{Bmatrix} \text{John and me} \\ \text{us} \end{Bmatrix}$ who <u>are</u> responsible.

e. It's you who <u>are</u> responsible.

f. It's $\begin{Bmatrix} \text{them} \\ \text{those two} \end{Bmatrix}$ who <u>are</u> responsible.

Pronouns in focus position are always in the objective case, and the verb in the clause is systematically <u>third</u> person.[2] The verb does not agree in person with the focus noun (or pronoun), but does agree in <u>number</u> with the focus noun. Thus:

(4) a. It's you who $\begin{Bmatrix} \underline{\text{does}} \\ \text{*do} \end{Bmatrix}$ this job. (Singular)

(But: You <u>do</u> this job.)

b. It's you who <u>do</u> this job. (Plural)

c. It's me who $\begin{Bmatrix} \underline{\text{does}} \\ \text{*do} \end{Bmatrix}$ this job.

(But: I <u>do</u> this job.)

d. It's us who <u>do</u> this job.

e. It's me that always $\begin{Bmatrix} \text{*get} \\ \underline{\text{gets}} \end{Bmatrix}$ the tough breaks.

(But: I always <u>get</u> the tough breaks.)

    f. It's us that always <u>get</u> the tough breaks.

How can we account for this complicated pattern of agreements?
Why is there number agreement but no person agreement? We
answer both these questions by deriving the cleft from the
pseudo-cleft sentence, since the pseudo-cleft sentence exhibits precisely the properties we want. For example, compare
the following with the above sets:

    (5) a. The one who <u>is</u> responsible is me.

       b. The one who <u>is</u> responsible is you.

       c. The one who <u>is</u> responsible is him.

       d. The <u>ones</u> who <u>are</u> responsible are $\left\{\begin{array}{l}\text{John and me}\\[4pt]\text{us}\end{array}\right\}$.

       e. The <u>ones</u> who <u>are</u> responsible are you.

       f. The <u>ones</u> who <u>are</u> responsible are $\left\{\begin{array}{l}\text{those two}\\[4pt]\text{them}\end{array}\right\}$.

       g. I am the one who $\left\{\begin{array}{l}\underline{\text{does}}\\[4pt]\text{*do}\end{array}\right\}$ this job.

       h. I am the one that always <u>gets</u> the tough breaks.

The relative clause of the pseudo-cleft sentence has a <u>third
person</u> head noun, <u>one</u>; in (d)-(f) we have the plural head noun
<u>ones</u>, and thus the plural verb in the relative clause.[3] Hence,
systematic third person marking, but agreement in plural marking. We account for the paradigm of Dialect I in a completely

natural manner. The complicated agreement pattern is given to us by regular rules of agreement -- no new rules are needed.

There are two other dialects I will discuss here, both of which are more complicated, and thus more interesting, than Dialect I. The first of these, Dialect II, has the following sort of pattern[4]:

(6) a. It is _I_ who _is_ sick.

    b. It is _me_ who(m) John is after.

    c. It is _I_ who _is_ being chased by Mary.

    d. It is _me_ who Mary is being chased by.

Verbal agreements in Dialect II are exactly those of Dialect I: consistently third person, with number agreement. Thus, just as with Dialect I, the proposed theory correctly predicts the agreement patterns. Dialect II differs from Dialect I with regard to case marking only. At first sight it seems to be the case that the focus pronoun agrees with the relative pronoun in case marking (assuming, of course, that relative pronouns are marked for case). However, this can't be right, since in Dialect II we have sentences such as:

(7) It is me who John says is sick.

where the relative pronoun would be marked nominative, being the subject of _is sick_, yet where the focus pronoun is accusative. Steve Anderson has suggested to me that the relevant generalization with regard to case marking is this: when there is a surface <u>subject</u> in the clause of the cleft sentence, the focus pronoun is marked accusative; when there is no surface subject, the focus pronoun is marked for nominative. Thus, the clauses of (6b), (6d), and (7) all have subjects (<u>John</u>, <u>Mary</u>, and <u>John</u>, respectively), hence the focus pronoun is marked as accusative. (6a) and (6c) have clauses in which there is no surface subject intervening between the focus pronoun and the verb of the clause, hence in these cases the focus pronoun is marked as accusative. I will assume that speakers of Dialect II differ from those of Dialect I in that they assign case to focus pronouns according to the surface generalization just stated.

We noted earlier that in Dialect I, focus pronouns are consistently marked for accusative. This suggests that speakers of Dialect I assign accusative case to focus pronouns on the basis of the fact that focus pronouns are in immediate post-verbal position (accusative case is used quite generally for items in post-verbal, or non-subject, positions). As G. L. Brook [1964, 152] points out:

> One of the most frequently discussed problems is whether to say <u>It is I</u> or <u>It is me</u>. The latter expression gained ground so quickly that it is now the

usual idiom, especially in colloquial speech... As early as the sixteenth century we find instances of the replacement of I by me, which probably arose because the pronoun here follows the verb, and the objective case generally follows the verb... Jesperson sums up what is happening to English pronouns: "On the whole, the natural tendency in English has been towards a state in which the nominative of pronouns is used only where it is clearly the subject, and where this is shown by close proximity to (generally position immediately before) a verb, while the objective is used everywhere else"... The opposition offered by prescriptive grammarians to the idiom It's me has had the result that many speakers have gained the impression that I is in some way more respectable than me.

Brook points out further that many speakers say:

(8) I sent for the man who had done it.

where the use of who is correct; on the other hand they say:

(9) I sent for the man whom I knew had done it.

These facts seem to correlate with the facts of Dialect II; where a noun subject intervenes between the relative pronoun and the verb phrase (had done it), the relative pronoun is marked for accusative. The speakers of Dialect II follow this rule with respect to focus pronouns.

What is crucial is that the proposed theory predicts correctly the facts of agreement for both Dialect I and Dialect II. I assume that the two dialects differ with respect to the rule(s) assigning case, where Dialect I assigns accusative case to post-verbal elements in general, and Dialect II has a more complicated rule based on a surface generalization concerning surface subjects in the clause.

Finally, let us examine Dialect III, which is more complicated than either of the previous two. Our data comes from Ross's paper on performative verbs [1968], where he points out the following sentences:

(10) a. It is I who $\left\{ \begin{array}{c} am \\ *is \end{array} \right\}$ responsible.

b. It is me who $\left\{ \begin{array}{c} *am \\ is \end{array} \right\}$ responsible.

Apparently, in this dialect, the case marking of the focus pronoun can be either nominative or accusative. The interesting feature of this dialect is that if the focus pronoun is nominative, then the verb of the clause agrees in person with it. Otherwise, just as with Dialects I and II, the verb is third person.

Since (10b) exhibits a pattern identical to that of
Dialects I and II, our theory accounts for at least part of
Dialect III with no changes made. The problem is how to account for (10a). Note that if the cleft sentence derives from
the pseudo-cleft sentence, then (10a) derives from a sentence
such as "the one who is responsible is me," not, "the one who
am responsible is me." The problem is how to account for the
agreement in person between the verb of the clause and the focus pronoun.

I suggest that if the pronoun happens to be marked as
nominative, then there is a low level rule in Dialect III
which changes the marking on the verb of the clause so that it
agrees with the focus pronoun. Why should Dialect III have
such a rule? I would suggest that speakers of Dialect III
produce sentences such as (10a) by analogy to the pattern associated with appositive clauses. When an appositive clause
is associated with a pronoun marked for nominative case,
there is person agreement between the verb of the clause and
the pronoun; however, when an appositive clause is associated
with a pronoun marked for accusative case, there is no agreement, but rather the verb of the clause is consistently third
person.[5] For example:

(11) a. I, who $\left\{ \begin{array}{c} \text{am} \\ \text{*is} \end{array} \right\}$ tall, was forced to squeeze into

that VW.

(11) b. He had the nerve to say that to me, who $\begin{Bmatrix} \text{has} \\ \text{*have} \end{Bmatrix}$

made him what he is today.

c. I, who $\begin{Bmatrix} \text{know} \\ \text{*knows} \end{Bmatrix}$ him, have come to hate him.

d. I wish she had said that to me, who $\begin{Bmatrix} \text{is} \\ \text{*am} \end{Bmatrix}$ sen-

sitive enough to understand these things.

These sentences are not particularly flowing, but the facts are intuitively quite clear. Furthermore, the above pattern is one which is found in all dialects, not just Dialect III.[6]

It is easy to see how the appositive paradigm could influence the cleft sentence pattern in Dialect III. Note that in surface structure the clause of the cleft sentence immediately follows the focus pronoun, and this is exactly the surface configuration of the appositive clause case (with the exception that the appositive clause is separated from the pronoun by a phonological pause):

(12) a. It is I who am responsible.

b. I, who am responsible, could never agree to that.

(12b), a construction shared by all speakers, provides a reasonable model for the pattern of (12a), as both constructions are virtually identical in surface structure. Therefore, it is suggested that Dialect III is derived basically just as Dialects I and II are, with (10b) being the basic form. The case marking rule apparently can assign nominative case optionally to focus pronouns, and if this happens then speakers of Dialect III "correct" the verbal agreement in the clause on analogy with the appositive pattern. Hence, the difference between the dialects lies in differing conditions on case-marking, with Dialect III containing a low level agreement rule.

We should note that it is not particularly surprising that such low level "correction" rules exist. While postulating such ad-hoc rules is to be avoided, we must take note of the fact that we deal here with a particularly troublesome area of English grammar, one which is often tampered with by grammar teachers in the schools. It is interesting to note that some speakers we have interviewed express complete confusion on the matter of proper pronominal and verbal forms in cleft sentences. It is in just this sort of situation that we would expect to find low level, ad-hoc corrections on the part of speakers, often in an attempt to speak "correct" English.

It has been suggested to me [by David Perlmutter,

personal communication] that the verbal agreement patterns in
cleft sentences might be accounted for in a completely different manner, namely, by claiming that there is a universal
principle that only nominative case can cause agreement of the
verb, and all other case forms cause the verb to remain in
third person (i.e. unmarked) form. Such a universal principle would account for the appearance of third person verb
forms in cleft sentences, and therefore, part of the evidence
for our proposal would be neutralized. However, this proposal
fails to explain certain crucial facts, namely, as we pointed
out for the sentences of (3) and (4), there is in fact number
agreement between the focus pronoun and the verb of the clause,
even though there is no person agreement. Hence, accusative
case pronouns are in fact causing certain agreements to occur.
The derivation from pseudo-cleft sentences shows why this pattern of partial agreement occurs.

3.2. Evidence from Reflexive Agreements in the Clause.

At this point I will consider another range of data, which
confirms the view I have presented. This evidence concerns
the agreement patterns which occur between the focus item and

reflexive pronouns in the clause. We find, in fact, that third person reflexive forms occur quite regularly. For example, the following are typical:

(13) a. It's not me that shaves himself with a straight razor.

b. Was it you that saw himself in the crystal ball?

c. It's me that cut himself so badly.

d. It's you and me who nearly drowned themselves out in the lake.

Sentences such as these once again indicate that the clause has a third person subject. As we would expect, the pseudo-cleft sentences exhibit just this pattern:

(14) a. The one who shaves himself with a straight razor is not me.

b. Was the one who saw himself in the crystal ball you?

c. The one who cut himself so badly was me.

d. The ones who nearly drowned themselves out in the lake are you and me.

Since we propose to derive the sentences of (13) from the sentences of (14), we are able to account for this pattern of reflexive forms in the cleft sentence. There is no other way that I see, which is not ad hoc, to account for the fact that

<u>himself</u> could co-occur with a first person focus pronoun.[7]

I have first presented the cases where the reflexive pronoun in the clause does not agree with the focus element, but
is systematically third person. This, I claim, is the basic
pattern. We must now consider cases where the reflexive pronoun does, in fact, agree with the focus pronoun, and we must
try to account for this agreement.

Let us begin with sentences in which reflexives occur in
the clause:

(15) a. It's me that cut myself.

    b. It's you that cut yourself.

    c. It's us who cut ourselves.

    d. It's me who has always kept $\left\{\begin{array}{l}\text{myself}\\\text{himself}\end{array}\right\}$ out of
       trouble.

    e. It's me who has to protect $\left\{\begin{array}{l}\text{myself}\\\text{himself}\end{array}\right\}$.

Such sentences are problematic for our view, since in the
pseudo-cleft the initial relative clause has a third person
head, and non-third person reflexives cannot be generated:

(16) a. *The one that cut myself is me.

    b. *The one that cut yourself is you.

    c. *The ones that cut ourselves are us.

    d. *The one who has always kept myself out of trouble
       is me.

(16) e. *The one who has to protect myself is me.

How, then, can we account for the fact that the reflexive pronouns agree with the focus in (15), if cleft sentences derive
from pseudo-cleft sentences?

I would suggest that the problematic reflexive forms in
(15) are spurious, and are not produced by the rule of reflexivization. To see this, notice that for one thing, in
(15d) and (15e) we have a syntactic paradox. That is, while
the reflexive pronoun agrees with the <u>first person</u> focus, the
finite verb is marked for <u>third person</u>. We do not have sentences such as:

(17) *It's me who have to protect myself.

Somehow, we must account for the fact that a first person reflexive co-occurs with a <u>third</u> person verb form.

Note further that the same pattern occurs in sentences
such as the following:

(18) a. I am the one who cut <u>myself</u>.

b. I am the one who <u>has</u> to protect <u>myself</u>.

These sentences are essentially inverted pseudo-cleft sentences: the focus element has been brought to the front of the
sentence, and the clause is sentence final. As with cleft
sentences, a first person reflexive can occur, but with <u>third</u>
person verb forms. Thus, we have the following situation:

(19) a. The one who has to protect $\left\{\begin{array}{l}\text{himself}\\\text{*myself}\end{array}\right\}$ is me.

    b. I am the one who has to protect $\left\{\begin{array}{l}\text{himself}\\\text{myself}\end{array}\right\}$.

    c. It is me who has to protect $\left\{\begin{array}{l}\text{himself}\\\text{myself}\end{array}\right\}$.

On the basis of (19) we see that it is when the clause follows the focus item in surface structure that the first person reflexive is possible. We must account for the appearance of this form with a third person verb form.

    I suggest that the reflexive forms in (15) and (18) arise
under certain surface structure conditions. To see this,
notice that in (15e), the version with myself answers a different question than the version with himself.[8] The version
with myself answers the following question:

    (20) a. Who has to protect you?

        b. It's me that has to protect myself.

        I am the one who has to protect myself.

Whereas the version with himself answers the question:

    (21) a. Who has to protect himself?

        b. It's me that has to protect himself.

        I am the one who has to protect himself.

Let us examine further the answers to questions such as (20a).
A very interesting pattern emerges:

(22) Who cut you?

 (i.) It was him who cut me.

 (ii) It was you who cut me.

 (iii) *It was me who cut me → It was me who cut

    myself.

 1.   He is the one who cut me.

 2.   You are the one who cut me.

 3.   *I am the one who cut me → I am the one who

    cut myself.

In answering this question, then, we would be forced into
uttering the sentence, "It was me who cut me;" hence, the
more acceptable form, "It was me who cut myself," or, "I am
the one who cut myself."

 It is interesting to note that there is no obvious syntactic reason why sentences (22.3) and (22iii) above should
be bad. The two pronouns are dominated by different S nodes
in deep structure, and this should be just as acceptable as
John is the one who cut me or It is John who cut me. We certainly would not expect reflexivization to apply here. It
seems reasonable to suppose that the repetition of phonologically identical person pronouns is somehow unacceptable
in surface structure. In fact, as we see, a succession of
identical person pronouns is unacceptable even when the pronouns are at different levels of embedding:

(23) a. Who was it that John believed hit you?

b. *It was me that John believed hit me.

*I am the one that John believed hit me.

(Cf. It was me that John believed hit Bill.)

While (23b) is quite unacceptable, it is somewhat more acceptable to have:

(24) ?It was me that John believed hit myself.

Thus, it seems to be the case that under certain conditions
(which I do not understand) a rightmost occurrence of a pronoun is changed to a reflexive pronoun under identity with a
pronoun on the left. This seems to relate to the fact that
there is a succession of phonologically identical personal
pronouns, and I suggest that the appearance of such reflexives
has the same status as the agreement rule we spoke of; that
is, a "correction" of sorts. The derivation, then, is as
follows:

(25) a. The one who has to protect me is me. → (Cleft
    Extraposition).

b. It is me who has to protect me. → (Reflexive
    Correction).

c. It is me who has to protect myself.

a'. I am the one who has to protect me. → (Reflexive
    Correction).

b'. I am the one who has to protect myself.

Once again, we note that such solutions -- i.e. low level correction rules -- are not, in general, attractive. Yet, as before, I think we ought to note that in this particular area of grammar it is not surprising to arrive at such solutions. Again we are dealing with an area subject to wide dialectal fluctuation, and an area, as we have noted, which some speakers avoid completely. It seems to me that the crucial fact in this case is the appearance of the _first_ person reflexive with the _third_ person verb form. The third person verb form indicates that the clause has a third person subject, and the first person reflexive would indicate that the clause has a first person subject. This paradox can be avoided by positing a first person _non-reflexive_ pronoun (which does not imply a first person subject for the clause), which at a late stage in the grammar is corrected by a trivial rule. This alternative eliminates the paradox while accounting for the syntactic gap created by the non-existence of sentences such as (25b) and (25a').[9]

3.3. Reflexives in Focus Position.

We have seen examples in which the clause contains reflexive pronouns which agree in person with the focus pronoun. There are also cases in

which a reflexive pronoun appears in focus position, and
agrees in person with a pronoun in the clause, just the re-
verse of the case we just discussed:

(26) a. It was myself that I shaved.

b. It was yourself that you cheated.

These, however, do not present problems for our view, since
these patterns are found in the pseudo-cleft sentence:

(27) a. The one that I shaved was myself.

b. The one that you cheated was yourself.

The Cleft Extraposition Rule will convert the sentences of
(27) to the cleft sentences of (26).

It is interesting to note that pseudo-cleft and cleft
sentences are parallel in yet another way, in that both contain instances of 'anomalous' reflexive forms in focus position. For example, consider the following sentences:

(28) a. It was himself that John claimed had been
cheated.

b. It was himself that John wanted Bill to describe.

(29) a. The one who John claimed had been cheated was
himself.

b. The one who John wants $\begin{Bmatrix} \text{Bill} \\ \text{Mary} \end{Bmatrix}$ to describe is
himself.

In the (a) sentences himself is coreferential with John, and
in the (b) sentences himself can be coreferential with either

<u>John</u> or <u>Bill</u>. Note, though that there are no non-clefted sentences corresponding to these:

(30) a. *John claimed that himself had been cheated.

b. *John wants $\begin{Bmatrix} \text{Bill} \\ \text{Mary} \end{Bmatrix}$ to describe himself.

(30a) is totally ungrammatical, and (30b) is starred since it has only one reading (where <u>himself</u> = <u>Bill</u>), and thus has lost the ambiguity in (28b) and (29b). We should note further that non-reflexive pronouns in focus position can only be interpreted in a non-coreferential way:

(31) a. *It was him that John claimed had been cheated.

b. *The one John claimed had been cheated was him.

(32) a. *It was him that John wanted Bill to describe.

b. *The one that John wanted Bill to describe was him.

The focus pronouns in these cases can only be interpreted as having outside reference. Thus a coreferential interpretation in these cases requires a reflexive pronoun.

We might possibly derive cases such as (28) and (29) by positing a pseudo-cleft source with emphatic reflexives, since these have the readings of (28) and (29):

(33) a. The one John claimed had been cheated was John himself.

(33) b. The one John wants Bill to describe is $\left\{\begin{array}{l}\text{John}\\\text{Bill}\end{array}\right\}$

himself.

A source such as (33) has the ambiguities in question, and accounts for the appearance of the reflexive pronoun. Further, application of Cleft Extraposition to the sentences of (33) will derive the cleft sentences in question.[10]

3.4. Evidence from Idiomatic Reflexive Constructions.

The next area which I will examine constitutes the final set of cases involving syntactic agreements. I refer to what we can call reflexive constructions; i.e., constructions which require identity between the subject and some possessive pronoun, and these include certain idioms, reflexive possessives, and certain verbs of perception. Regarding idioms, note that there is a required identity in the following:

(34) a. I held my breath for five minutes.

b. I found my way home.

c. I made up my mind.

It is impossible to have any other pronominal forms -- the identity is obligatory. However, as we would expect, in cleft sentences the pronouns are in third person form:

(35) a. Was it you that held <u>his</u> breath for five minutes?

    b. It was only me who could find <u>his</u> way home in the storm.

    c. It was me that made up <u>his</u> mind before anyone else.

I do not know the facts for other dialects, but in my own, agreement cannot occur. Sentences such as, "Was it you that held your breath for five minutes?" are anomalous since they imply contrasts such as *"Or was it John that held your breath for five minutes?" These facts show, once again, that the clause has a third person subject. The pseudo-cleft sentence gives us just the right paradigm:

(36) a. Was the one who held his breath for five minutes you?

    b. The only one who could find his way home in the storm was me.

    c. The one who made up his mind before anyone else was me.

    (Cf. *The one who made up my mind before anyone else was me.)

The same facts hold for reflexive possessives. There is an obligatory identity:

(37) I hit $\begin{Bmatrix} \text{my own} \\ \text{*his own} \end{Bmatrix}$ father.

Yet, in the cleft sentence (and in the pseudo-cleft) we have no agreement, but systematic third person:

(38) a. It's me that hit $\begin{Bmatrix} \text{his} \\ *\text{my} \end{Bmatrix}$ own father.

b. The one who hit $\begin{Bmatrix} \text{his} \\ *\text{my} \end{Bmatrix}$ own father is me.

Finally, with certain verbs of perception we have similar obligatory identities:

(39) I felt a spider crawl up $\begin{Bmatrix} \text{my} \\ *\text{his} \end{Bmatrix}$ leg.

But once again we get third person forms in the cleft sentence:

(40) a. It wasn't me who felt a spider crawl up his leg.

b. The one who felt a spider crawl up his leg was me.

Agreement does not occur in cleft or pseudo-cleft sentences, at least in Dialect I, and this is especially clear if we add a negative element:

(41) a. *It wasn't me who felt a spider crawl up my leg.

b. *The one who felt a spider crawl up my leg wasn't me.

To sum up, we have presented evidence from three general areas, namely, verbal agreement patterns, reflexive agreement patterns, and agreement patterns in reflexive construction. The evidence presented indicates that the clause of the cleft

sentence has a third person head, and agreements within the
clause, with few exceptions (such as (15)), are for third person. We show that these patterns are just those found in the
initial relatives of the pseudo-cleft, and therefore we can
predict the range of agreement patterns for the cleft sentence
on the basis of such patterns in the pseudo-cleft sentence.
Having presented this evidence, we will turn now to a more
detailed look at the specific derivation proposed.

4. The Deep Structure Source for Cleft Sentences

In our discussion so far we have used pseudo-cleft sentences with bound relatives as examples in the derivation of
cleft sentences. However, we have stated that cleft sentences
do not derive from these, but rather from pseudo-cleft sentences which have free relatives, in particular, those formed
by the extraction rule. Thus, instead of derivation (42),
derivation (43) is the proper derivation for cleft sentences:

(42) a. ┌The one who Nixon chose was Agnew.

     b.   It was Agnew who Nixon chose

(43) a. ⌐[it [Nixon chose Agnew] be Λ]

b. ⌐[it [Nixon chose who] be Agnew]

c. ⌐[it [who Nixon chose] be Agnew]

d. [it is Agnew [who Nixon chose]]

Our claim is that cleft sentences derive ultimately from structures such as (43a).

An immediate and obvious advantage of derivation (43) is
that it provides a natural source for the dummy _it_ of the
cleft sentence, since free relatives (including those formed
by the extraction rule) arise from NPs which dominate [it-S].
When the S node is extraposed, _it_ is left behind, and if
extraposition does not apply, _it_ is deleted, as it is in
general. With a derivation such as (42), however, it is not
clear that the dummy _it_ has any natural source, and we face
further the problem of eliminating the lexical head of the
relative when the clause is extraposed. Hence, (42) is more
complicated.

Secondly, there are semantic problems associated with
postulating pseudo-clefts with bound relatives as the source
for cleft sentences. For example, compare the following sentences:

(44) a. The place where I found John was in the garden.

b. Where I found John was in the garden.

c. It was in the garden that I found John.

(44b) and (44c) are synonymous, but they are not in turn synonymous with (44a). (44a) tells us where a certain place is located, while (44b) and (44c) tell us where John was located. This can be seen even more clearly in sentences such as:

(45) a. The place where John was was in the garden.

b. Where John was was in the garden.

where, again, the first tells us of the location of a certain place, while the second tells us of the location of John.[11] Thus, the lexical head of the bound relative makes an additional independent semantic contribution to the total meaning of the sentence, which is not found in sentences with free relatives.

To consider another example, note that in certain cases it is impossible to have a lexical head for the relative. In some instances, the presence of the lexical head causes an ill-formed copula statement. For example:

(46) a. *The place where John went was to Boston.

b. Where John went was to Boston.

c. It was to Boston that John went.

(46a) is ill-formed since the basic equation is anomalous, i.e. [the place was to Boston]. In other words, we can not specify the place in question by equating it with a prepositional phrase. In other instances, the relative clause can

apparently have no lexical head at all. Compare the following examples:

(47) a. *The way young men are registered is in this
atmosphere.

b. ?How young men are registered is in this atmosphere.

c. It is in this atmosphere that young men are
registered.

(47a) is completely ungrammatical, and there is apparently no
other lexical head possible for this case. (47b) is more
acceptable, but at best awkward. (47c) is completely acceptable. This case, in fact, leads us to the strongest evidence for derivation (43), namely, cases in which prepositional phrases are the foci of cleft sentences. As we shall see,
only derivation (43) can generate such cases.

5. Evidence from the Derivation of Prepositional Phrases

The most problematic cases for any analysis of cleft sentences are those such as the following:

(48) a. It is in this atmosphere that young men are
registered.

(48) b. It was to John that I gave the book.

    c. It was by the police that John was beaten.

    d. It was out of spite that he kissed her.

    e. It was with Howard Johnson that we met first.

We have already seen that there are no pseudo-cleft sources for most of these sentences.[12] In attempting to account for such sentences we are therefore faced with the problem of finding a source which allows us to generate prepositional phrases in focus position, which further accounts for the lack of prepositions in the clause. In addition we must explain why only _that_ clauses, and not WI-clauses, are permissible with these cases. We should also note that certain of these clauses would be ungrammatical in isolation (for example the clause _that we met first_ in (48e)), and we must explain this. All of these factors are explained by deriving such sentences according to derivation (43). Consider, then, the phrase markers:

(49) a.

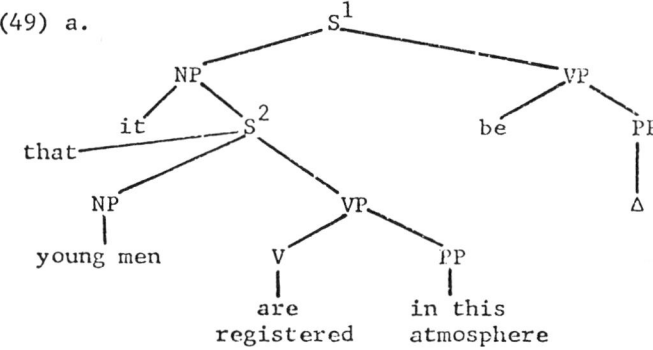

(49) b.

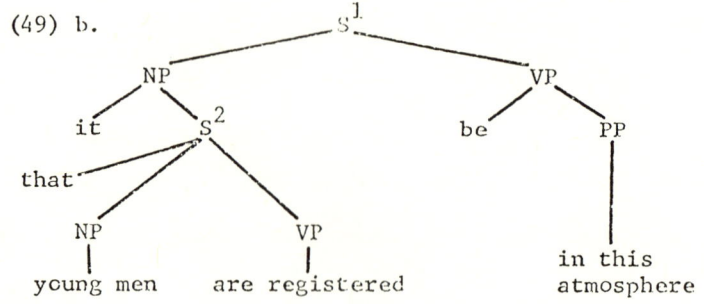

c.

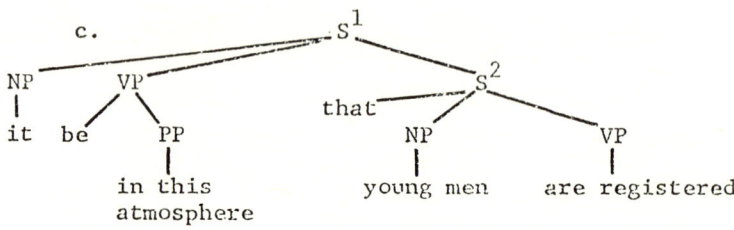

(49a) constitutes the deep structure input to the Extraction
Rule, which extracts the PP in this atmosphere and places it
in predicate position, forming the derived structure (49b).
Note that no pro-form is left behind for the prepositional
phrase. This is a crucial fact, since it means that when such
PPs are extracted, one should be left with that-clauses, since
the complementizer that (e.g. in S^2 of (49b)) will not be replaced by a WH pro-form.

The crucial fact here is that there are no syntactic
pro-forms for prepositional phrases such as those in (48).
To see this, note that noun phrases can be pronominalized in
various ways (and thus have representative pro-forms), however,

many prepositional phrases cannot be pronominalized. This can
be seen in the fact that there are no pro-forms in English
which could occupy the following kinds of slots:

(50) a. I gave the book to John, and Bill gave the car

_____

b. John was arrested by the police, and Bill was

beaten _____

That is, there is no pro-form which could stand for the
phrase to John, or by the police, and the only pronominalization possibility is to pronominalize the NPs within the prepositional phrases (e.g. to him, by them). Along with the
fact that such prepositional phrases cannot be pronominalized
goes the fact that they cannot be questioned. One way to
illustrate this is to note that the prepositional phrases,
(b), cannot answer the questions, (a):

(51) a. How are young men registered?

b. *In this atmosphere.

(52) a. How was John beaten?

b. *By the police.

In other words, our claim is that English grammar contains a
gap in its system of syntactic pro-forms. As a consequence
of this, in structures such as (49b), no pro-form is left behind in place of the extracted prepositional phrase, resulting
automatically in clauses headed by the complementizer that.

The Cleft Extraposition Rule maps (49b) onto (49c), and thus
the problematic cleft sentences such as those of (48) can be
derived.

We should note here that we have stated that _many_ prepositional phrases do not have syntactic pro-forms. This
equivocation is due to certain considerations involving
locative and temporal phrases which seem to indicate that
some prepositional phrases might indeed have syntactic pro-
forms. We refer here to the locative _where_ and _there_ along
with the temporal _when_ and _then_. First of all, note that
prepositional phrases can apparently be pronominalized by
there and _then_:

(53) a. I went _to Boston_ and John went _there_ too.

b. I left _at 5 o'clock_ and Bill left _then_ too.

Furthermore, _where_ and _when_ in questions seem to stand for
prepositional phrases, and we can see this by noting the
possibility of answering such questions with prepositional
phrases:

(54) a. Where did John go?

b. To Boston.

(55) a. When did John leave?

b. At 5 o'clock.

Given these considerations, it appears to be the case that
such prepositional phrases have pro-forms. If this is the

case, then the extraction rule could indeed leave behind pro-
forms for certain prepositional phrases.[13]

If the considerations of the above paragraph are valid,
then derivations such as the following should be possible:

(56) a. [[it [that- John went to Boston]] be   △]

b. [[it [that- John went where]]   be to Boston]

c. [[it [where John went]]   be to Boston]

Since the prepositional phrase to Boston is one of those
which apparently can be replaced by a pro-form, (56b) can be
formed from (56a). Note, however, that if such derivations
are possible, we must prevent sentences such as (56c) from
undergoing Cleft Extraposition since we do not get cleft sentences of the form:

(57) *It was to Boston where John went.

In order to derive the appropriate cleft sentences, we
must impose the following restrictions:

(58) a. Structures with initial WH-clauses may not
   undergo Cleft Extraposition.[14]

b. Structures with initial that-clauses must undergo Cleft Extraposition.

Furthermore, we must then stipulate that the extraction rule
optionally leaves behind a pro-form for phrases it extracts.
If the extraction rule happens to leave behind a pro-form,
then pseudo-clefts with initial WH-clauses are formed. If

the extraction rule does not leave behind a pro-form (as, for example, when there is none to leave behind), then it will result in structures with initial that-clauses, which must obligatorily undergo Cleft Extraposition. Note that it would be necessary in any event to stipulate that pro-forms are left behind optionally, since even when NPs are extracted, it is possible to have that-clauses:

(59) It was John that I saw.

Since we argue that that-clauses arise from simple deletion of some item (i.e. with no pro-form left), this means that no pro-form has been left behind for sentences such as (59).

To sum up the possibilities in the derivation of cleft sentences, consider the following examples:

(60) a. [[it [that- I saw John]] be Δ]

b. [[it [that- I saw   ]] be John]

c. [it be John [that I saw]]

(61) a. [[it [that- I saw John]] be Δ]

b. [[it [that- I saw who]] be John]

c. [[who I saw] be John]

(62) a. [[it [that- John went to Boston]] be Δ]

b. [[it [that- John went where]] be to Boston]

c. [[where John went] be to Boston]

(63) a. [[it [that- John went to Boston]] be Δ]

b. [[it [that- John went   ]] be to Boston]

(63) c. [it be to Boston [that John went]]

(64) a. [[it [that- we met with HoJo]] be Λ]

b. [[it [that- we met   ]] be with HoJo]

c. [it be with HoJo [that we met]]

(61) and (62) represent derivations in which a pro-form has
been left behind for the item extracted, and these ultimately
end up as pseudo-cleft sentences with initial WH-clauses.
(60) and (63) represent derivations in which no pro-form has
been left behind, and these cases obligatorily become cleft
sentences. (64) represents a derivation in which there is
no pro-form which can be left behind, thus it can only become
a cleft sentence.[15]

To sum up this section, we have attempted to show that
the derivation of cleft sentences with prepositional phrases
in focus position represents evidence in favor of deriving
cleft sentences ultimately from deep structures posited in the
Extraction Theory. We have shown that, given the Extraction
Theory, there is a straightforward means of deriving prepositional phrases in focus position. Further, we can explain
why no preposition appears in the clauses, and why, in fact,
the clause itself contains a gap (cf. (64c)). Finally, we
note that sentences such as (48) can have only that-clauses,
and no WH-clauses, for the reason that no pro-forms can be
left behing when the extraction rule operates. Hence, there

could be no possibility of forming WH-clauses. (This would leave unexplained, however, potentially exceptional cases listed in note 13, as well as (56)). These considerations, then, provide support for deriving cleft sentences from pseudo-cleft sentences (i.e. ultimately from structures under-lying pseudo-cleft sentences).[16]

6. Restrictions on Items which can Appear in Focus Position

In discussing the syntax of cleft sentences, we should note that there are restrictions on the sort of items which can appear in focus position. For most speakers interviewed, the items which can appear in focus position are noun phrases (including verbal complements which have heads) and preposi-tional phrases:

(65) a. It was John that I saw.

b. It was
$$
\begin{cases}
\text{in the garden} \\
\text{at 5 o'clock} \\
\text{out of spite} \\
\text{by pinning her down} \\
\text{because he loved her}
\end{cases}
$$
 that John kissed

Mary.

(65) c. It's the fact that Mary hates me that I can't

bear.

d. It's John's driving that bothers me.

e. It's Sirhan's assassination of Kennedy that

astounds me.

It is not possible, however, to have verb phrases in focus

position, or verbal complements without heads:

(66) a. *It was go that John did.

b. *It was for John to go that I wanted.

c. *It's that the world is round that I believe.

At first glance these facts appear to be unsystematic; however,

J. Emonds has provided a principled explanation for the facts

of (65) and (66) within what he terms the Structure Preserving

Framework.[17]

Recall that the extraction theory posits a deep struc-

ture source for pseudo-clefts which has an empty predicate.

The node Pred, however, is an abbreviation for the nodes

which can possibly appear after the copula. In fact, in deep

structure, the syntactic source for pseudo-cleft sentences

contains in predicate position major category nodes such as

NP, PP, VP, and so on, which dominate the dummy symbol [Δ].

Further, within the Structure Preserving Framework, the deep

structure which ultimately becomes a cleft sentence must also

contain an S node at the end of the VP. Thus, for a sentence such as (65a) we have the deep structure source:

(67)

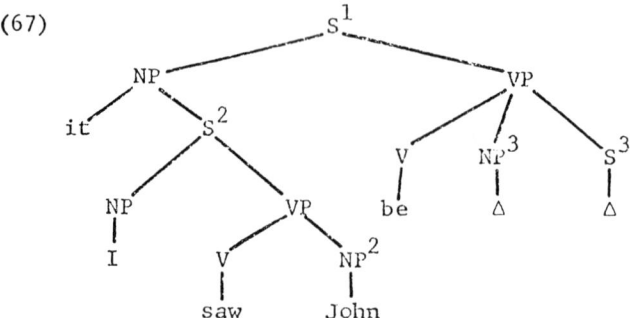

In (67), the NP dominated by the verb phrase, NP^3, dominates the dummy symbol [Δ], and this NP can be replaced by an extracted NP (hence "filling" the empty predicate). No other kind of constituent can replace this NP, since, on the Structure Preserving hypothesis, movement rules can move some item X into a position where the phrase structure rules generate the node X. In other words, movement rules can move an NP only where the phrase structure rules of English generate the NP node. Thus, after extraction we would have:

(68)

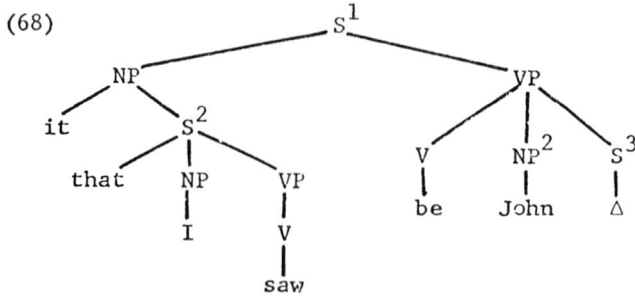

At this point the Cleft Extraposition rule must apply. Once

again, movement rules can move the $\underline{S}^2$ node only to where the phrase structure rules generate $\underline{S}$ nodes. In this case, S^2 can be moved to the position where the phrase structure rules have generated S^3. This results in:

(69)

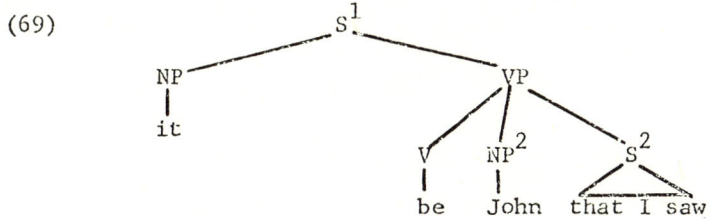

In short, both the Extraction Rule and the Cleft Extraposition Rule, being movement rules, can only move constituents of type X where the phrase structure rules provide nodes of type X.

With this brief background (for detailed discussion, see Emonds [1970]), we can now appreciate how the Structure Preserving Hypothesis predicts that sentences such as those of (66) are not possible. That is, for such sentences to be possible, the deep structure would have to contain VPs of the following sort:

(70) a.

Thus, (66a) would require a structure such as (70b), since it has the form _(it) be+go+that John did_, in other words, _it V+VP+S_. Sentences such as (66b,c) would require structures

such as (70a), since these are of the form be+S+S. The crucial fact, however, is that the English phrase structure rules
provide no VP expansions such as those of (70) (as argued in
detail by Emonds). There are expansions such as that of (68)
(i.e. V+NP+S, cf. force+John+to leave), and expansions such as
V+PP+S (e.g. mention+to John+that S), and thus we can have
cleft sentences with NPs and PPs in focus position. However,
sentences such as (66) are blocked because the phrase structure rules of English do not provide the proper VP expansions
which would allow such sentences to be generated.[18]

7. Further Extensions

The extraposition process we have posited here appears to
be more general than we have stated it. That is, we have
assumed that it operates only on certain output structures of
the Extraction Rule. However, there appear to be base-generated structures to which it also applies. Consider sentences
such as:

(71) a. My job is to keep order here.

b. The task of syntax is to describe sentences.

c. My feeling is that John should stay.

When the items connected by the copula are reversed, there is a drop in acceptability:

(72) a. ?To keep order here is my job.

b. ?To describe sentences is the task of syntax.

c. ?That John should stay is my feeling.

However, notice that there are sentences such as those of (73), which are synonymous with those of (71):

(73) a. It's my job to keep order here.

b. It's the task of syntax to describe sentences.

c. It's my feeling that John should stay.

If we assume that the sentences of (72) have the following structure:

(74) a. [[it [(for me) to keep order here]] is [my job]]

b. [[it [(for it) to describe sentences]] is [the task of syntax]]

c. [[it [that John should stay]] is [my feeling]]

then we can assume that Cleft Extraposition operates on the embedded sentences leaving _it_ behind. These, then, are analogous to the cleft sentences we have discussed in that the embedded clauses have no WH-pro-forms, but rather have complementizers such as _that_ (and her _for-to_ as well). Thus, the rule extraposes an initial clause in a copula construction (i.e. specificational statement) which has no WH pro-forms. In this way, it is not limited to cleft sentences.

8. Summary

The objective of this chapter has been to provide an account of the syntactic derivation of cleft sentences. We argue that the cleft sentence must derive from pseudo-cleft sentences (ultimately from the deep structure provided by the extraction theory). The evidence adduced in support of this proposal is evidence from formal (i.e. syntactic) considerations, not from semantic considerations. The first general sort of evidence presented deals with syntactic agreement patterns, and we show that these can be predicted, given the proposed derivation for cleft sentences. The second sort of evidence has to do with the derivation of prepositional phrases in focus position in cleft sentences. This area provides support for the extraction theory, and for the proposal to derive cleft sentences in the manner of (43).

FOOTNOTES TO CHAPTER 2

1. Even though the discussion in this chapter centers on sen-
    tences such as (1), the analysis is, of course, intended
    to extend to all cleft sentences, in particular to pairs
    such as the following:

    (i)   What John bought was a car → It was a car that
           John bought.

    (ii)   Where I saw John was in Boston → It was in
           Boston that I saw John.

    (iii) When John left was at three o'clock → It was at
           three o'clock that John left.

    (iv)   Why John did that was to irritate me → It was to
           irritate me that John did that.

    (v)   How John did that was by standing on a ladder →
           It was by standing on a ladder that John did
           that.

2. For my own speech, _who_ and _that_ are completely interchangeable as relative pronouns of the clause in cleft sentences. There are dialects in which there is a difference in acceptability in many cases between the use of _who_ as opposed to _that_; however, as far as I know, this should make no difference to the analysis proposed here.

3. The examples used in the first section of this chapter have pseudo-cleft sentences with bound relatives, rather than free relatives, even though we claim that cleft sentences do not derive from these particular forms. The reason for this is solely the fact that some speakers do not find acceptable pseudo-cleft sentences with free relatives, such as (ii)-(v) in footnote (1). Since it makes no difference in these sections which form is used (i.e. both have the properties needed), we naturally use the form acceptable to most speakers.

We should make clear, however, that free relatives do have the properties necessary to derive cleft sentences. Consider, for example, the following input structure:

(3) (cont'd.)

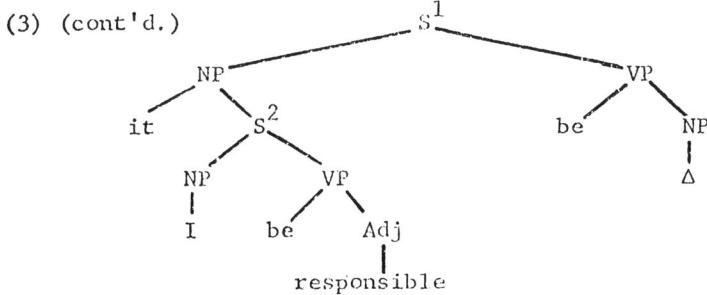

The Extraction Rule can apply to extract the subject of the embedded sentence, the NP I. When this is placed in predicate position, the pro-form who is left behind, since who is the pro-form for human nouns. This results in the following:

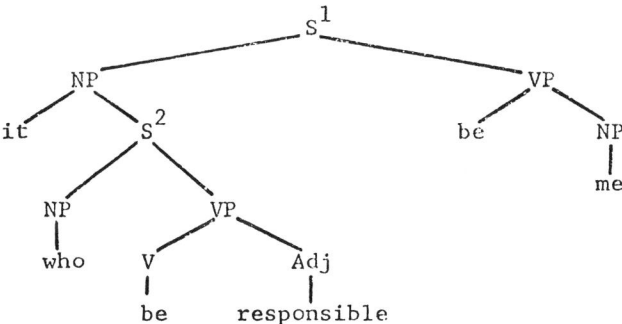

Note that the pro-form who is syntactically third person, and when the verb agreement rule applies be of S^2 is inflected to agree with the subject, who, and ends up as the third person is. Note further that if a plural subject had been extracted, the pro-form would be marked as syntactically plural, and the verb would end up as the third

(3) (cont'd.)

person plural _are_. (Since most speakers find pseudo-cleft
sentences with initial _who_ clauses unacceptable (as mentioned in Chapter 1), these must obligatorily undergo
Cleft Extraposition to become cleft sentences. See note
16).

4. ⌐ I am grateful to Steve Anderson and Morris Halle for
pointing out the facts of Dialect II.

5. This fact was pointed out to me by Peter Culicover, to
whom I am grateful for discussion on this section. It
should be made clear that by stating that certain cleft
sentences in Dialect III are produced "by analogy to"
appositive clauses, I wish to express two facts; namely,
(a) that the patterns found in both constructions (with
regard to case marking) are identical, and (b) that the
appositive clause construction is "primary" since it is
found in _all_ dialects, while the cleft sentence agreement
pattern of Dialect III is found only in that one dialect.

6. It is not possible to discuss the analysis of appositive
clauses in this paper; however, it is interesting to note
one further fact: appositive clauses associated with

(6) (cont'd.)

accusative pronouns can begin with head nouns such as <u>the</u>

<u>one</u>, <u>the person</u>, etc., however, this is not possible when

such clauses are associated with nominative pronouns:

  (i)   He had the nerve to say that to me, the one who

        has made him what he is today.

  (ii) *I, the one who loves her, will always defend

        her.

7. Note also that these facts hold for Dialect II, as well.

    Steve Anderson points out interesting cases such as the

    following:

        It is I who in spite of himself is sick.

8. This fact was pointed out by Ray Jackendoff, and is quoted

    in Ross [1968, footnote 52].

9. The matter is not as simple as we have stated it, however.

    J.R. Ross has pointed out to me cases in which a succession

    of identical person pronouns is unacceptable, but in which

    reflexive forms are equally unacceptable:

  (i)   It's me who thinks Mary loves $\left\{ \begin{array}{l} \text{*me} \\ \text{*myself} \end{array} \right\}$.

Only the <u>third</u> person non-reflexive pronoun is acceptable

(9) (cont'd.)

in this environment:

    (ii) It's me$_i$ who thinks Mary loves him$_i$.

It seems to be the case that the occurrence of the reflexive is most acceptable when there is no subject NP
within the clause in which the reflexive occurs (as in
(25c) and (25b')).

10. The matter of "anomalous" reflexives is discussed further
in Chapter 5, where it is shown that such forms cannot be
interpreted as normal reflexives, since they form the <u>foci</u>
of their containing sentences. We show that interpretation
of pro-forms changes significantly depending on whether
the pro-form is focal or non-focal.

11. The distinction between (44a) and (44b) is manifested in
another difference as well, namely that the tense of the
copula need not agree with the tense of the verb in the
clause in (44a):

    (i) The place where John was <u>is</u> in the garden.

    (ii) *Where John was is in the garden.

As we point out in Chapter 3, non-agreement in tense indicates a non-specificational use of the copula. In the
case of (i) above, we have a locative use of the copula in

(11) (cont'd.)

the statement [the place is in the garden].

12. (48a) and (48b) have no sources for reasons pointed out in
    connection with (47a,b) and Chapter 1, (79). There are no
    corresponding pseudo-cleft sentences for (48c) and (48d);
    (48e) has as the closest possible source the sentence:

    (i) (the one) who we met with first was Howard
        Johnson.

    where, just as with (79) of Chapter 1, there is a problem
    in generating the PP in focus position, and eliminating
    the preposition of the clause.

13. The matter of pro-forms for prepositional phrases forms a
    complicated area of English grammar. For example, on the
    basis of examples such as (54) and (55), one might also
    argue that why and how also can represent prepositional
    phrases:

    (i) Why did John go?

        For no reason.

    (ii) How did John do that?

        By standing on a ladder.

    However, there are no analogues of there and then (i.e.
    non-WH pro-forms) for why and how, as we see from the

(13) (cont'd.)

blanks in the following:

    (iii) a. I did it for that reason and Bill did it

          _____ too.

        b. John did it by standing on a ladder, and Sam

          did it _____ too.

There is no pro-form which replaces the phrase <u>for that</u> <u>reason</u>, and no pro-form which replaces the phrase <u>by stand-</u> <u>ing on a ladder</u> (although it may be marginally acceptable to use the pro-form <u>thus</u>). There are, in other words, un-systematic gaps in the set of pro-forms for prepositional phrases.

The situation is complicated even more by the fact that in certain cases the preposition can actually appear with some of these forms. Thus, consider:

    (iv) a. Where did John go <u>to</u>?

        b. Where did John come <u>from</u>? (cf: *Where did John come?)

    (v) a. *I went to Boston and Sam went to there also.

        b. I came from Boston and John came <u>from</u> there too.

Given sentences such as (ivb) and (vb) it is questionable whether <u>where</u> (and <u>there</u>) are pro-forms for prepositional phrases, since the preposition in these cases must appear.

(13) (cont'd.)

It is not our purpose to embark on a study of such forms.
The only point is that if in fact there are pro-forms for
some prepositional phrases, then such pro-forms could be
left behind by the extraction rule.

14. There is one exception to this principle, namely, clauses
which have who:

    (i) a. It was John who I gave the book to.

        b. It was John to whom I gave the book.

Thus, we must allow such clauses to extrapose. (See note
16.)

15. It should be noted that there are some restrictions on the
kinds of prepositional phrases which can be extracted and
placed in focus position. For example, note sentences
such as:

    (i) a. ?It is about Nixon that he always talks.

        b. *It is about Nixon that he always reads books.

Note, however, that the facts represented in (i) do not
have to do specifically with the derivation of cleft sentences, but are rather part of a more general phenomenon,
and the restriction in question can be related to restrictions on movement rules in general. Thus, compare the

(15) (cont'd.)

sentences of (ii) with those of (i):

(ii) a. ?About Nixon he always talks.

b. *About Nixon he always reads books.

We see that when such prepositional phrases are moved by the rule of Topicalization, the sentences are just as un-acceptable as the cleft sentences of (i). Thus, whatever restriction is involved here, it is a restriction on move-ment rules in general, and not a special restriction on the extraction rule.

16. The restrictions listed in (58) remain, at this writing, as specific restrictions on Cleft Extraposition. It would be desirable, of course, if such restrictions were appli-cable in a wider range of cases, or if they followed from more general principles. However, at the present time it is not clear to me whether such restrictions generalize to other areas of the grammar.

Note that for (58a), the situation is complicated by seemingly erratic facts and dialect differences. For most speakers I have interviewed, it is the case that extraposed WH phrases are unacceptable. The only exception consists in extraposed who clauses; however, as we have mentioned, this correlates with the fact that pseudo-cleft sentences

(16) (cont'd.)

with initial <u>who</u> phrases are judged as unacceptable, or at least less acceptable than pseudo-clefts with other WH-clauses. We can relate these facts by assuming that initial <u>who</u>-clauses obligatorily undergo extraposition.

Other speakers I have interviewed accept not only <u>who</u> clauses, but also other WH-clauses in extraposed position. For example, J.R. Ross has pointed out to me sentences such as:

(i)   It was in the garden where I saw John.

(ii) It was on the beach where I first met her.

Ross further points out, however, that if the focus prepositional phrase is a directional phrase, then such extraposition is unacceptable:

(iii) *It was to Boston where he went.

Thus, for some speakers extraposition may apply to WH-clauses besides <u>who</u> clauses, with restrictions of various sorts. It can be said, however, that for most speakers (58a) holds true with the single exception noted.

17. For a detailed exposition of the Structure Preserving Framework see J. Emonds [1970]. For the discussion of cleft sentences in particular, see Emonds [1970, section 3.2.1].

18. I leave as an open question whether adjectives can appear
    in focus position. While (i) seems unacceptable, (ii)
    seems to be better:

    (i) It's tall that John is.

    (ii) It's idiotic that John always manages to be.

CHAPTER 3

THE SEMANTIC INTERPRETATION OF CLEFTED SENTENCES AND THE
SEMANTIC REPRESENTATION OF FOCUS-PRESUPPOSITION RELATIONS

1. Objectives

In the last two chapters we have discussed the syntactic
derivation of clefted sentences, and we have seen that these
can derive from two deep structure sources. In this chapter
we attempt to show how it is possible that a single surface
structure deriving from two deep structure sources can be assigned only one semantic reading. We first point out that
the dual source for clefted sentences cannot be associated
with semantic ambiguities, and that ambiguities which are
found in clefted sentences are in fact part of more general
phenomena. We then show that the two deep structure sources
from which a single clefted surface structure can derive are
semantically equivalent, and thus that no semantic difference
results from the fact that the deep structures are formally
distinct. Finally, we discuss focus-presupposition relations,

and show that since these are determined by factors of surface
structures, a single clefted surface structure will receive
only one set of such relations. Thus, since the deep structures are semantically equivalent, and since other aspects of
interpretation are determined from the single surface form,
clefted sentences deriving from two sources receive only one
reading.

The discussion of focus in this chapter is particularly
central. First of all, this is important given that the deep
structures posited by the Extraction Theory contain an empty
[Δ], and give no indication as to which constituent(s) may be
the focus. Since this is the case, we must show that this
deep structure source causes no semantic problems, and that
for independent reasons focus-presupposition relations must be
determined from factors of surface structure, not deep structure. For this reason, we discuss focus in some detail, and
in the course of this discussion we propose a semantic notation for focus-presupposition relations. Therefore, this
chapter has a broader purpose than that of discussing clefted
sentences in particular, namely, to show what a representation
of focus-presupposition relations would look like. We justify
this representation on the basis of arguments from the structure of discourse, as well as 'logical scope'. Further, in

Chapter 4 we present additional justification for this notation. Thus, in discussing these broader issues, we will show
that there is no need for deep structures to include any indication of focus-presupposition relations, and that a distinction in deep structure source for clefted sentences need not
lead to any semantic distinctions.

2. Basic Factors in the Interpretation of Clefted Sentences

2.1. Specificational vs. Predicational. In the course of
our discussion of the interpretation of clefted sentences, we
will have occasion to refer to two fundamental senses of the
copula, namely, the specificational sense as opposed to the
predicational sense. These two senses of the copula are illustrated in simple examples such as:

(1) a. The first candidate for the trip to Mars is Spiro
       Agnew.

    b. The first candidate for the trip to Mars is short
       and fat.

There is an intuitively clear distinction between these two
sentences, in that the first sentence identifies, or specifies,
some entity, while in the second sentence given qualities are

predicated of some individual. An obvious difference between
these two is that the first sentence tells us who the candidate is, while the second sentence does not. From the second
sentence, we do not know who the candidate is, we only know
what he is, that is, what qualities he has. Clefted sentences
are always specificational: that is, the clause of the clefted
sentence contains a semantic variable (represented by the WH
word), and this variable is specified by the post-copular item.
Hence, of the following two sentences, (2a) is a clefted sentence, while (2b) is a predicational sentence:

(2) a. (the one) who we chose to go to Mars was Spiro
       Agnew.

    b. (the one) who we chose to go to Mars was short
       and fat.

Once again, sentence (2a) tells us who was chosen (i.e. the
variable has been given a value), however, from (2b) we do not
know who has been chosen, we only know that, whoever it was,
he has certain qualities of being short and fat. Thus, the
variable is not specified in (2b). This fundamental distinction is manifested in various syntactic and semantic differences, which can in fact be used as diagnostic tests for the
two senses. First of all, we note that in a specificational
statement, the order of items connected by the copula can be
reversed, while in a predicational statement such reversal

yields an ungrammatical sentence. Thus, compare the sentences
of (2) with those of (3), in which reversal has taken place:

(3) a. Spiro Agnew was the one who we chose to go to
Mars.

   b. *Short and fat was the one who we chose to go to
Mars.

The specificational sentence (2a) (and also (1a)) may be reversed, as shown by (3a), however, the predicational (2b)
may not.

A second basic difference between the two senses rests
with the fact that predication is a semantic relation which
admits comparison and modification of degree, while specification is a semantic relation which in some sense implies
uniqueness, and there can be no modification of degree.
Thus, one can say that someone is very fat, or somewhat tall,
or that someone is taller than someone else. However, one
cannot say that Jones is somewhat the man who robbed the bank,
or that he is more the man who robbed the bank than he is the
man who lives on the corner. Jones either is or is not the
man who robbed the bank, and there can be no sense of modification of degree.

Predicational and specificational senses are also distinguished in interesting ways in pseudo-cleft sentences themselves. Consider a pseudo-cleft sentence such as:

(4) What he is is tall.

This is a specificational statement (i.e. the item tall is not predicated of the subject NP <u>what John is</u>, but rather is a specification of the variable represented by <u>what</u>) and this can be seen from the fact that (4) allows reversal:

(5) Tall is what John is.

Even though (4) is itself a specificational statement, the sentence from which it is formed must be a <u>predicational</u> statement. Thus, from (6a) we can form the pseudo-cleft sentence (7a), however, from (6b) we cannot form (7b):

(6) a. He is tall.

b. He is the man who robbed the bank yesterday.

(7) a. What he is is tall.

b. *What he is is the man who robbed the bank yesterday.

Thus, for predicational statements there are corresponding pseudo-cleft sentences which have the form <u>what X is</u>, however, for specificational statements there are no such pseudo-cleft forms. This provides another differentiation between the two senses.

2.2. Referential vs. Non-Referential. In order to explain
the facts manifested in (7), we must look at cases with predicate nominals. So far we have discussed predicational statements in terms of sentences which contain adjectives, however,
predicate nominals, as well, appear in predicational statements:

    (8) a. John is a fool.

       b. *A fool is John.

       c. John is more a fool than he is a pedant.

       d. What John is is a fool.

According to the tests we have established, (8a) is clearly
a predicational statement. The difference between a predicational statement such as (8a) and a specificational statement
such as (6b) rests with the fact that the post-copular NP of
(6b) is referential, while the post-copular NP of (8a) is
non-referential (following the terminology of Kuno [1969]).
As Kuno points out, noun phrases such as a fool in (8a) are
non-referential, in the sense that they are understood to
have no specific referent in the universe of discourse. Thus,
the speaker who uses the phrase a fool in (8a) does not denote
any individual in the world by using that phrase. On the
other hand, the noun phrase the man who robbed the bank
yesterday in (6b) is in fact understood as denoting a specific

individual, i.e. an individual can be picked out by the use of that phrase.[1]

The difference in referentiality, however, is also manifested in certain syntactic differences. The primary difference, as Kuno points out, is with respect to pronominalization: non-referential NP's may be pronominalized by <u>which</u>, even when they are marked as animate. However, referential NPs may not:

(9) a. He is a gentleman, <u>which</u> you are not.

b. *Jones is the man who robbed the bank yesterday, <u>which</u> Smith is not.

Similarly, in pseudo-cleft sentences, non-referential NPs may be replaced by <u>what</u>, however, referential NPs may not:

(10) a. What he is is a gentleman.

b. *What he is is the man who robbed the bank yesterday.

Conversely, referential NPs may be replaced by <u>who</u>, while non-referential NPs may not:

(11) a. *Who he claims to be is a gentleman.

b. Who he claims to be is the man who robbed the bank yesterday.

Thus, the difference between referential and non-referential NPs shows up in the difference between possible syntactic pro-forms which may replace such NPs (when the NPs in question

are animate). Referential NPs may be represented pronominally
by who, and non-referential NPs may be represented by which
or what.[2] Kuno provides an example, in fact, where both what
and which appear:

(12) What you need is a good wife, which you don't have.

For such reasons, then, we see why (7b) is not possible: the
pro-form what, in the initial clause, has incorrectly replaced
a referential NP.[3]

2.3. Further Distinguishing Features. Another distinction between specificational and predicational senses we can
cite is the fact that certain tense agreement phenomena influence the interpretation of the copula with respect to these
two senses. That is, it has been noted often that in pseudo-
cleft sentences the tense of the copula must agree with the
tense of the verb in the clause. Thus, consider:

(13) a. What you are holding in your hands is a small
        brown butterfly with spots on its wings.

    b. What you are holding in your hands was a small
        brown butterfly with spots on its wings (once).

    c. What you are holding in your hands will be a
        small brown butterfly with spots on its wings.

As we see, only (13a) informs us as to precisely what is being held; (13b) does not specify what is being held, but merely indicates that the object in question once had certain properties; (13c) as well does not specify the object in question, but states certain properties which the object will come to possess. It is interesting to note that only (13a) allows reversal, while reversal in (13b) and (13c) causes ungrammaticality:

(14) a. A small brown butterfly with spots on its wings is what you are holding in your hand.

b. *A small brown butterfly with spots on its wings was what you are holding in your hand.

c. A small brown butterfly with spots on its wings will be what you are holding in your hand.

This suggests that (13b,c) are predicational, while (13a) is specificational. Because the focal items in (13b) and (13c) do not in fact specify the variable in the clause, these are therefore not considered as 'clefted' sentences, in the sense in which we have discussed that term.

It should be noted that while the phenomenon illustrated by the sentences of (13) has been viewed in terms of tense agreement, it is in fact part of a deeper phenomenon. Consider, for example, sentences such as:

(15) a. His old job was building radars at Lincoln Labs.

b. *His old job is building radars at Lincoln Labs.
The use of the adjective old in his old job denotes a former
state of affairs, now no longer extant. Given this interpretation, it is not possible to speak of a former state of
affairs as if it still existed; however, this is just what is
implied in sentence (15b), where the present tense of the copula is used. Such examples, which do not involve agreement
of verb tenses as such, indicate that specificational statements imply a temporal congruence of the entities referred to
by the NPs in such statements. It is clear, then, that agreement in tenses in (13) is a superficial reflex of a deeper
phenomenon.

As a final example of the distinction between predicational and specificational senses, we note that this distinction forms the basis for ambiguous sentences such as the following:

(16) What he wants his next wife to be is fascinating.
In the predicational sense, the adjective fascinating is taken
as modifying the entire complex subject, what he wants his
next wife to be. In this sense, the variable of the clause is
not specified, and thus we do not know what it is he wants
his next wife to be, we only know that it strikes the speaker
as fascinating. On the other hand, in the specificational
sense, (16) can be paraphrased as follows:

(17) He wants his next wife to be fascinating.

Furthermore, under reversal, (16) has only a specificational sense:

(18) Fascinating is what he wants his next wife to be.
The two senses are distinguished in an interesting way in the following, where on the specificational reading (19) represents a contradiction, however, on the predicational sense (19) is consistent:

(19) What John wants his next wife to be is fascinating -- believe it or not, he wants her to be dull and boring.

Within the framework we have developed so far, there is a straightforward means of distinguishing these senses. We can account for the ambiguity in sentences such as (16), in that such sentences can derive either from a predicational source in the base, or from a transformational source:

(20)

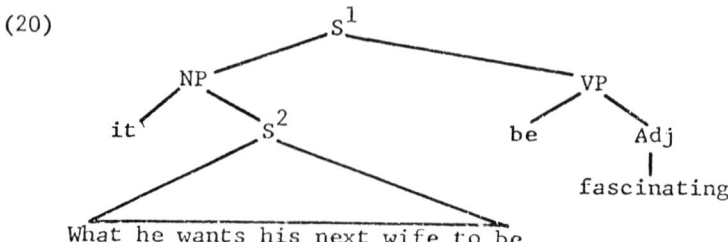

(21)

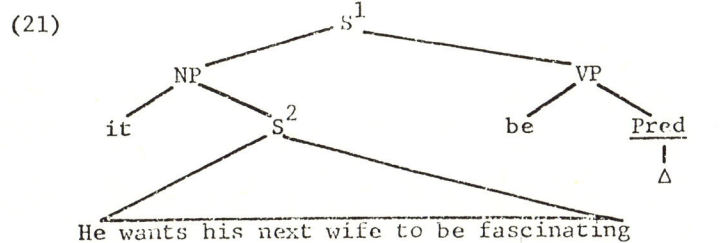

$$S^1$$

NP   VP

it S^2 be   Pred

Δ

He wants his next wife to be fascinating

The predicational sense of (16) has a representation such as
that shown in (20), the source in the base, and thus it has
a representation of the same form as simple predicational
statements (e.g. "The idea is fascinating"). Such a representation correctly shows the 'scope' of the adjective fascinating to be the entire complex subject NP. The representation for the specificational sense is (21), which ultimately undergoes the Extraction Rule. This representation correctly indicates that the scope of the adjective fascinating
is not the entire complex NP which dominates S^2, but rather
is the NP his next wife within the embedded sentence.[4]

The unitary surface structure (16) is thus differentiated
at the level of deep structure. On the assumption that grammatical relations are determined in deep structure, (20) will
be interpreted as a predicational statement (i.e. the grammatical relation holding between subject and predicate is that
of predication, since the structure is of the form NP-be-Adj).
The deep structure predicate of (21), on the other hand, is
semantically empty. (As we discuss in section 4.1, the

element [Δ] carries no semantic interpretation). Thus, at the deep structure level (21) does not receive a specificational interpretation. Rather, the specificational interpretation associated with the pseudo-cleft which derives from (21) (in this case, (16)) is assigned to it as part of its focus-presupposition relations. (This is discussed throughout section 6. See in particular note 18.) Thus, the ambiguity of (16) is accounted for in the following way: it can be generated as a basic predicational statement (i.e. (20)); or, as a specificational statement, it is generated as (21) and receives its specificational interpretation as part of its focus presupposition relations, in a manner discussed in section 6.

The distinction between predicational and specificational senses is a fundamental aspect of the interpretation of copula sentences, and therefore one of the crucial aspects in distinguishing clefted sentences from other copula sentences. In discussing semantic representations in later sections, we will need to use certain notation to represent various meanings, and we will use the symbol [=] to refer to the semantic relation of specification, and we shall simply use the orthographic spelling [is] as a technical symbol for the relation of predication.[5] Thus, as a first rough approximation, we can represent the senses of (16) as:

(22) a. What he wants his next wife to be is fascinating.

     b. What he wants his next wife to be = fascinating.

We will develop such rough representations further as we go

along.

3. Semantic Ambiguity in Clefted Sentences

Before discussing semantic representations, we should

discuss further certain aspects of the semantic interpreta-

tion of clefted sentences, namely, the existence of certain

ambiguities. It is clearly important to investigate the ques-

tion of ambiguities thoroughly, since we wish to determine

whether a semantic notation must provide formal expression

for ambiguity, if any is present. Furthermore, given the con-

clusions we have reached as to the syntax of clefted sentences,

the matter of ambiguity becomes significant: it is important

to determine whether any semantic ambiguity can be systemati-

cally associated with the syntactic derivational ambiguity of

clefted sentences. We will show that while various ambiguities

can be found in clefted sentences, the ambiguities in question

cannot be associated with the specific derivation of clefted

sentences as such. Rather, the ambiguities in clefted

sentences are reflexes of much more general phenomena, and thus can not in fact be associated with a dual syntactic source for clefted sentences.

We have already discussed certain ambiguities in sentences with predicate adjectives, and we will now consider ambiguities in sentences with nominals in post-copular position. For example:

- (23) What he threw away was a valuable piece of equipment.

This sentence is ambiguous in a way analogous to sentences such as (16). It has a specificational sense, in which the phrase a valuable piece of equipment is taken to have a specific referent in the universe of discourse. In this sense we know exactly what it was that was thrown away, and this sense allows reversal:

(24) A valuable piece of equipment was what John threw away.

On the other hand, (23) can have a predicational sense, in which the NP a valuable piece of equipment is not understood to have any specific referent. In this sense we do not know what was thrown away; we only know that, whatever it was, it has certain qualities, as described in the predicate phrase. Note that in this sense, the tense of the copula need not agree with the tense of the verb in the clause:

(25) What he threw away is a valuable piece of equipment.

At first glance, it would appear as if the ambiguity of (23) should be accounted for in a manner analogous to (16), namely, by differentiating the two senses on the basis of the two sources for pseudo-cleft sentences, as follows:

(26)

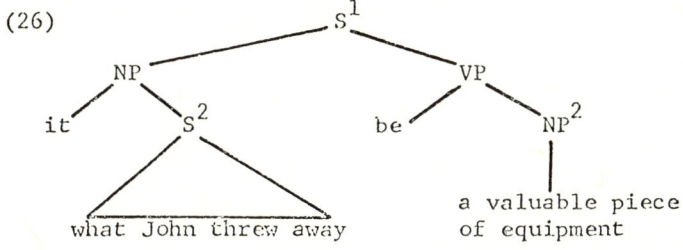

(27)

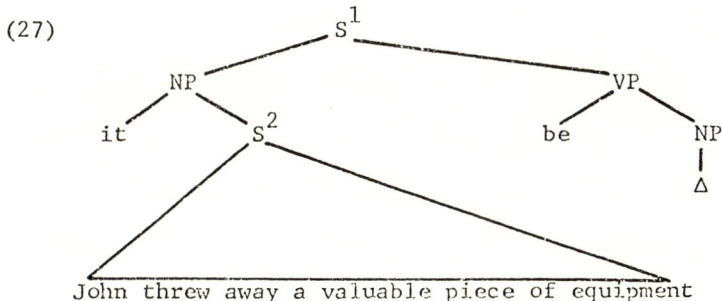

Thus, (26) would represent the predicational sense, while (27) would represent the specificational sense, as before.

However, this approach would be mistaken in several ways. Consider, for example, a sentence such as:

(28) What John threw away was the valuable piece of equipment.

This sentence is understood unambiguously as specificational,

i.e. the underlined NP in (28) is unambiguously referential.
The crucial point here is simply this: sentence (28) could
arise from either (26) (as NP^2), or from (27) (in the position of the underlined NP embedded in S^2). The phrase structure rules allow NPs to be generated after the copula (as in
(26)), as well as in positions such as that of the NP in S^2
of (27). Such NP positions can be expanded either as indefinite NPs or definite NPs, and therefore, (28) could arise
from either (26) or (27). The difference between (26) and (27)
can not be used to explain the specificational/predicational
ambiguity of (23), since each source in turn can generate
sentences which are either predicational or specificational.

The ambiguity in (23) is not specifically associated with
the derivation of pseudo-cleft sentences, as such, but is a
function of the semantic nature of the noun phrase a valuable
piece of equipment. The distinction between the predicational
and specificational senses is a function of the referentiality
of this particular NP, rather than any property of the deri-
vationof clefted sentences.

The view that the ambiguity in question is not associated
specifically with the derivation of clefted sentences is
greatly strengthened by noting that the same ambiguity shows
up in non-clefted sentences as well. Consider, then:

(29) He threw away a valuable piece of equipment.

This sentence is ambiguous in just the way sentence (23) is, and the two senses can be resolved by addition of appropriate contexts:

(30) a. Jones is an idiot -- he threw away a valuable piece of equipment, which I certainly could use right now.

b. We don't know what the secret agent threw away -- we only know that he threw away a valuable piece of equipment.[6]

The ambiguity of (29), like that of (23), is a function of the referentiality of the NP a valuable piece of equipment: when the NP is taken as being referential, the sentence is understood to have a specificational sense, and when the NP is taken to be non-referential, the sentence is understood as having a predicational sense. Such examples show that the ambiguity in question is not associated with the specific derivation of clefted sentences. Thus, the ambiguity in (23) is not accounted for by positing a dual source (as in (26) and (27)), but rather it is a function of the general phenomena of referentiality of nominal expressions.

Even if we leave aside such considerations, however, positing a dual source such as (26)-(27) to account for the ambiguity of (23) would be mistaken on purely syntactic grounds. Suppose that (26) were the source for the

predicational sense of (23), and (27) the source for the specificational sense, and furthermore, that special conditions
were placed on such structures to insure that each structure
would represent either one or the other sense, but not both.[7]
If this were the case, then there would be no reason to expect that referential and non-referential NPs should have the
same, or even similar, formal syntactic distributions. It
would be a total accident that both sorts of NPs appear in the
same syntactic environment. This would be an absurd consequence. The general formal distribution of NPs is not in any
way governed by the referentiality of NPs, which is why we
find both referential and non-referential NPs in the same
syntactic environments. Thus, positing a dual source to account for ambiguities such as that in (23) is mistaken on
several grounds.

Returning to sentences such as (23), we note that such
examples can be multiplied freely. For example, in a paper
by E. Clifton [1969] cases such as the following are discussed:

(31) What I drew was a piece of trash.

This can be paraphrased either as, "There is a piece of trash
which I drew (sketched)", or roughly as, "My drawing was quite
poor". Once again, the ambiguity is predicated on the basis
of whether or not the object NP is taken as referential. And
again, it is mistaken to assume that the ambiguity can be

associated with the specific derivation of clefted sentences,
since the very same ambiguity appears in non-clefted sentences:

(32) I drew a piece of trash.

The ambiguity can be resolved by changing the main verb:

(33) I wrote a piece of trash.

(34) I photographed a piece of trash.

Thus, in (33) only the non-referential interpretation of the
object NP is compatible with the selectional restrictions of
the verb write; in (34) only the referential interpretation is
compatible with the selectional restrictions of the main verb.
It is clear, then, that the specificational/predicational
ambiguity in sentences such as (23), (29), (31) and (32) is
a function of certain properties of noun phrases, and not a
function of the derivation of particular syntactic forms.

We have been considering cases with indefinite focal
NPs, however, clefted sentences with definite focal NPs also
manifest certain ambiguities, not entirely unrelated to the
specificational/predicational sort. Consider, for example:

(35) What he told us was the answer.

This can be taken as meaning either that he intentionally
told us what he recognized as the answer, or on the other
hand, that he told us something, and that we, perhaps at a
later time, label what he told us as the answer. Note that

the former sense is preferred under reversal:

(36) The answer was what he told us.

while the latter sense is preferred when there is non-agreement of tenses:

(37) What he told us _is_ the answer.

Could this ambiguity be grounds for positing some dual source
for the pseudo-cleft? Once again, this cannot be the case
since the ambiguity is not restricted to clefted sentences.
The very same ambiguity appears in simple non-clefted sentences
such as:

(38) He told us the answer.

The ambiguity can be resolved by addition of appropriate contexts:

(39) a. After we tortured him for 5 hours, he finally
       told us the answer.

    b. When he told us Richard Nixon's birthdate, he
       didn't realize it, but he told us the answer.

The ambiguity is a function of certain properties of reference, namely whether both speaker and hearer are committed
to a given description, or whether just the speaker alone is
committed to a description. Again, this has nothing to do
with the particular derivation of clefted sentences.[8]

In Chapter 1 we noted that certain clefted sentences
could only be derived in the base, while others could only

be transformationally derived. However, for a subset of
pseudo-cleft sentences we noted that either syntactic source
is possible. Here we have attempted to show that no semantic ambiguity can be associated specifically with this
duality of syntactic source. This leaves us, therefore, with
the situation that a single surface structure with a single
semantic reading can derive from two deep structure sources:

(40)   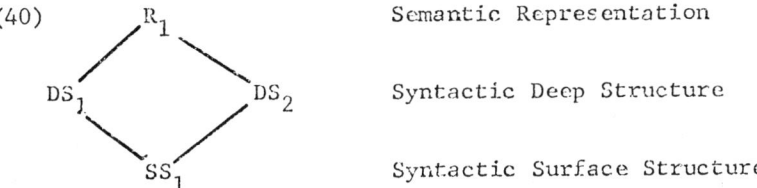   Semantic Representation

                        Syntactic Deep Structure

                        Syntactic Surface Structure

In the sections that follow we will consider the semantic
representation of clefted sentences, and we will show why
(40) is possible, given certain assumptions about the nature
of semantic interpretation.

4. The Semantic Interpretation of Clefted Sentences

In examining the question of the semantic representation
of clefted sentences, several relevant questions arise. Most
obvious, of course, is the question of how a single surface
structure which derives from two formally distinct deep

structures is assigned one semantic reading. Since an unambiguous surface structure expresses one set of grammatical relations, if it derives from more than one deep structure source it must be the case that each distinct deep structure expresses just the same set of grammatical relations: the deep structure sources in question, though formally distinct, are semantically equivalent. We will show that this is the case.

After discussing deep structure aspects of the interpretation of clefted sentences, we discuss those aspects of interpretation determined at the surface structure level, i.e., focus-presupposition relations. We extend and modify in various ways the general principles for interpreting focus first discussed by Chomsky [1969], and we propose a semantic notation for representing focus-presupposition relations.

4.1. Deep Structure Considerations. Consider a pseudo-cleft sentence such as the following:

(41) What we must avoid is the draft.

Sentences such as (41) can derive from either of the following sorts of deep structures:

(42)

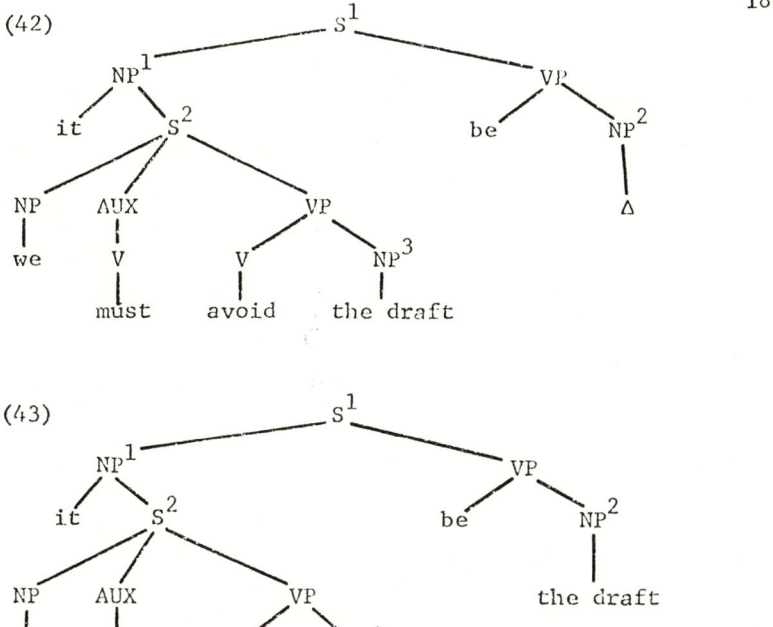

(43)

We assume that grammatical relations are determined at the
level of deep structure. Since sentence (41) expresses unambiguously one set of grammatical relations, the same set
of grammatical relations must be assigned to both (42) and
(43). In fact, (42) and (43) are semantically equivalent for
reasons which we now discuss.

Beginning with S^2 of both (42) and (43), semantic rules
operate to determine the grammatical relations expressed in
this embedded sentence. The only semantic difference between

(42) and (43) at the level of S^2 is that (42) has a fully specified NP as object in S^2 (i.e. NP^3), while (43) has a less semantically specified NP in this position (i.e. a pro-form). Thus, while the embedded sentences of both (42) and (43) express the same set of grammatical relations, the semantic information they contain differs to the extent that NP^3 of (43) is less specified than NP^3 of (42).

There is an additional semantic operation in S^2 of (43), since, by convention, a pro-form receives semantic features projected by the selectional restrictions of the items with which the pro-form enters into selectional relations (cf. Katz and Postal [1964]). Thus, the pro-form in (43) receives semantic features projected by the object selectional restrictions of the verb avoid. Further, we assume, as discussed in Chapter 1, that the semantic features of the pro-form become associated with the larger NP which dominates the free relative.[9] These operations on S^2 are not carried out by particular interpretive rules, but are rather general semantic conventions, which form part of the universal definition of 'pro-form' and 'free relative'. This completes the relevant semantic operations on S^2.

Moving now to the level of S^1, consider first deep structure (42). We assume, with Emonds [1970], that empty nodes at the level of deep structure are ignored by interpretive rules, i.e. are semantically empty and contribute neither to the semantic ill-formedness nor well-formedness of a sentence at this level. They do not make any semantic contribution in the determination of grammatical relations or selectional violations, and are simply left as uninterpreted items. This means that the predicate of (42) is semantically empty. Recall now that the semantic interpretation of the copula is a function of the semantic nature of the items which it links. (See note 3.) For this reason, the copula in (42) cannot receive an interpretation, since the post-copular NP is semantically empty. Thus, at the deep structure level the cleft superstructure, represented as the matrix sentence S^1, is semantically empty. The semantic information which (42) expresses is just the semantic information of the embedded sentence, and no more.

Consider now S^1 of (43). Since grammatical relations are determined at the deep structure level semantic rules operate on (43) to mark it as a specificational statement. (It is at this point that such sentences would be marked as semantically deviant if the semantic features of the items connected by the copula did not agree, as discussed in Chapter 1. Here, however, the relevant features are in agreement (i.e. the NP the draft has those semantic features which are shared by possible objects of the verb avoid)). Note, however, that the important point here is this: since NP^1 is marked with the features of the embedded pro-form, and since NP^1 is then specified as NP^2, the net effect of these two factors is that the pro-form of S^2 ends up specified as the post-copular NP^2.

Once we see this, it is clear that (42) and (43) express the same semantic information. On the level of S^2, (42) and (43) differ only in that (43) contains a less specified object NP. Thus while (43) tells us that something must be avoided, (42) tells us specifically that the draft must be avoided. However, this semantic difference is neutralized at the level of S^1. Since the pro-form of (43) is specified as NP^2 at the level of S^1, the two deep structures (42) and (43) become semantically equivalent, for the same reason that the following formulations are semantically equivalent:

(44) avoid the draft

(45) avoid x, x = the draft

The essential difference between (42) and (43) is that (42) expresses the grammatical relation between verb and object as (44), while (43) expresses this relation, in effect, as in (45). Since these are logically equivalent formulations, the deep structures in question are semantically equivalent.

<u>4.2. Surface Structure Considerations.</u> The determination of grammatical relations forms only one aspect of the total semantic representation of a sentence. Projection rules operating on the level of deep structure, assign a partial semantic reading to a sentence. This deep structure reading contains the basic semantic proposition(s) expressed by the sentence, in that it represents the basic logical ('grammatical') relations found in the sentence. The deep structure reading of a sentence, in a clear sense, represents the basic logical information of the sentence, the semantic information which has bearing on the truth conditions of a sentence.

The basic information expressed in sentences, however, can be 'processed' in various ways by speakers. Certain portions of the information expressed can be highlighted or made semantically prominent, while other portions can be treated as redundant or presupposed. Certain portions of the information may be novel with respect to a given discourse, while other portions may be known to both speaker and hearer. In other words, given a basic logical proposition (i.e. deep structure reading), there are various modes in which the information contained in the proposition can be presented.

Broadly speaking, while the logical propositions

expressed by sentences are determined by factors of deep structure, the information 'processing' (or mode of presentation) is determined by factors of (phonetically interpreted) surface syntactic structure.[10] Such factors of surface structures as surface constituent structure, placement of intonation center, and shape and scope of intonation contours, determine the manner in which semantic information associated with given deep structures is processed as to semantic prominence, novelty, and so forth. The system of focus-presupposition relations comes under this general area of information processing, that is, it is a semantic system determined by factors of surface structures. Recent research, especially that of Chomsky [1969] and Jackendoff [1969], has shown that factors of intonation (e.g. the placement of the intonation center) are used to split up and categorize the semantic information of a sentence into focus (generally speaking, 'novel' information) and presupposition.

5. 'Focus' and 'Presupposition'

Chomsky [1969] defines focus as a technical term referring to a constituent of a sentence (where constituent is defined in such a way that the entire sentence may be a constituent) which contains the intonation center, i.e. the position of highest pitch and stress. The term is intended to cover both cases where a constituent receives normal sentence final stress, as well as constituents which receive so called emphatic stress. The presupposition of a sentence, in the sense in which Chomsky uses it, is defined in terms of the notion of focus in the following way: the presupposition is a statement derived by replacing the focus of a sentence with an appropriate semantic variable. For example, consider the sentences:

(46) a. MITCHELL urged Nixon to appoint Carswell.

b. Mitchell urged NIXON to appoint Carswell.

c. Mitchell urged Nixon to appoint CARSWELL.

The difference which we intuit in such sentences is a function of the shifting focus-presupposition relations. In (46a) Mitchell is the focus (being the constituent which contains the intonation center). The presupposition of the sentence (in the sense of 'presupposition' used by Chomsky) is the statement derived by replacing the focus with a variable. If we replace the focus constituent Mitchell with a variable, x, we derive the presupposition x urged Nixon to appoint Carswell. Turning to (46b), according to our definitions the constituent Nixon forms the focus (since it forms the intonation center), and replacing this constituent with a variable we derive the presupposition <u>Mitchell urged x to appoint Carswell</u>. Finally, in (46c), we interpret the focus as the constituent <u>Carswell</u>, and we derive the presupposition <u>Mitchell urged Nixon to appoint x</u>. In sum, the term 'focus' in one sense refers to a constituent which contains the intonation center; the term 'presupposition' is defined in terms of focus, and, by definition, is always a statement which contains a variable.

As semantic notions, focus and presupposition form part of the semantic reading of a sentence. As for the general interpretation of these notions, if we examine the sentences listed in (46), we intuitively understand the focus constituent in each case to have a semantic prominence with respect to the rest of the sentence. The focus constituent is set apart from the surrounding material by its higher stress, and the speaker singles out this constituent as being semantically special and important. As Halliday describes focus [1967, p. 204]:

> (47) "Information focus is one kind of emphasis, that
> whereby the speaker marks out a part (which may be
> the whole) of a message block as that which he
> wishes to be interpreted as informative. What is
> focal is 'new' information; not in the sense that it

cannot have been previously mentioned, although it is often the case that it has not been, but in the sense that <u>the speaker presents it as not being recoverable from the previous discourse</u>. The focal information may be a feature of mood, not of cognitive content, as when the speaker confirms an asserted proposition; but the confirmation is itself still 'new' in the sense intended... The focus of the message, it is suggested, is that which is represented by the speaker as being new, textually (and situationally) non-derivable information." [Emphasis mine -- AA]

Hence the general interpretation of the notion 'focus' is that portion of a sentence which is 'new' (in the sense of (47)), informative, "interesting", and semantically prominent with respect to the surrounding material. This "surrounding material" is relatively low-key, semantically non-prominent material, and forms the presupposition. The use of the term <u>presupposition</u> reflects the intuitive feeling that non-focal material is generally indeed presupposed by the speaker to be known to the hearer, and thus is material which is non-informative.

As we see from the examples of (46), semantic prominence is correlated with phonetic prominence. The interpretive principle implied by such examples can be stated as follows:

> (48) The portion of the semantic reading of a sentence
> which is to be assigned as the <u>focus</u> is that portion
> of the reading which is associated with any consti-
> tuent of the surface syntactic structure which con-
> tains the intonation center. For every possible
> focus there is a presupposition which is the pro-
> position derived by replacing the focus material
> with appropriate semantic variables.

This is, in effect, the interpretive principle for focus
given by Chomsky [1969]. We will make the principle more explicit in the course of developing a semantic notation for
focus and presupposition.

Before this can be discussed meaningfully, however, we
must first approach the question of the linguistic significance of these notions. Are the notions of 'focus' and 'presupposition' indeed part of the semantic representation of
sentences? If so, how do we justify this position? Secondly,
if focus-presupposition relations are part of the semantic
representation of sentences, what evidence indicates that
these relations are determined by properties of surface structures? We turn to these issues at this point.

5.1. The Linguistic Significance of the Notions 'Focus'
and 'Presupposition'.   It has become clear from recent research that focus-presupposition relations play a crucial
role in several areas of the grammar.   In particular, such
relations are crucial in explicating the structure of well-
formed discourse (e.g. in formulating notions such as "appropriate response"); and secondly, in the broad area of so-
called 'logical scope' of negation, questioning, and adverbial
elements.   We shall review here in a general fashion research
presented by S.R. Anderson [forthcoming, a], Chomsky [1969],
and Jackendoff [1969].

5.1.1. The Notion of Focus and the Structure of Discourse.   To begin with, consider the fact that we understand
the sentences of (46) to answer different questions.   That is,
the sentences of (46) answer, in respective order, the following questions:

   (49) a. Who urged Nixon to appoint Carswell?

       b. Who did Mitchell urge to appoint Carswell?

       c. Who did Mitchell urge Nixon to appoint?

If we pair-off questions with answers, we note that (46a)

answers only (49a), (46b) answers only (49b), and so on.
This is the only natural pairing possible, since all other
possibilities are judged to be unacceptable. For example,
the following do not form a natural question-answer pair:

(50) a. Who urged Nixon to appoint Carswell?

b. Mitchell urged Nixon to appoint CARSWELL.

If we look for an explanation for these intuitively clear
facts, it is striking that there is no recourse to deep structure differentiation: all three sentences of (46) express the
same logical proposition, i.e. express just the same grammatical relations. If this is the case, why are not all three acceptable as answers for any of the given questions of (49)?
To answer this, consider the question (49a). The speaker who
asks this question already has certain information given to
him, which he presupposes, namely that someone urged Nixon to
appoint Carswell. He requests certain novel information,
namely, the identity of the person who urged Nixon. An
analogous presuppositional analysis can be given for the other
questions as well: the WH-word represents a request for novel
information, while the surrounding material is presupposed to
be given. When searching for appropriate responses to such
questions, we look for answers which share the presuppositions
of the questions, and further which indeed specify the semantic "gap" of the question, i.e. which provide novel

information. If we examine the sentences of (46), we note that the constituents which contain the intonation center are interpreted as representing novel information, while the surrounding material is taken as non-novel, already given information. In short, we match answers with questions if they share presuppositions, and if the focus of the answer is a specification of the question word of the question.

To illustrate the presuppositional analysis of the sentences we have discussed in a more revealing fashion, we can convert the sentences of (49) and (46) into the following paraphrase forms:

(51) a. Someone urged Nixon to appoint Carswell -- who?

b. Someone urged Nixon to appoint Carswell, namely, MITCHELL.

(52) a. Mitchell urged someone to appoint Carswell -- who?

b. Mitchell urged someone to appoint Carswell, namely, NIXON.

(53) a. Mitchell urged Nixon to appoint someone -- who?

b. Mitchell urged Nixon to appoint someone, namely, CARSWELL.

One does not, of course, hear such question-answer pairs in everyday speech. The point, however, is that such paraphrase forms allow us to compare and check questions and answers to determine in a general fashion which answers form natural responses to which questions. The definition of 'natural' response can then be stated generally as follows:

(54) A 'natural' response to a given question must share the presupposition of the question, and must contain as focus an item which specifies the semantic variable of the question.

The paraphrase forms of (51)-(53) allow us to apply principle (54) in a straightforward manner, since such paraphrase forms isolate foci and presuppositions clearly. Insofar as the notions of focus and presupposition allow us to explain pairing phenomena, they are linguistically significant.

The sentences of (46) are examples in which the intonation center shifts within one given surface structure, thereby causing a corresponding shift in focus-presupposition relations. Consider now the case of a set of distinct surface structures which all derive from the same deep structure source. Even though such surface structures are cognitively synonymous, insofar as the surface constituent structure of each is distinct, each variant determines a distinct (but partially overlapping) set of focus-presupposition relations. Such examples are discussed in Chomsky [1969], but to take an example which has been raised recently (by Lakoff [1969]) we note the following pair of sentences:

(55) a. He called up a girl who he had met in Chicago.

    b. He called a girl up who he had met in Chicago.

These sentences are identical at the deep structure level (having as a source the structure underlying (55a)). (55b) is derived if the structure underlying (55a) is operated on by the rules of Particle Movement and Relative Clause Extraposition (cf. Ross [1967]). The surface constituent structure of these two sentences is different, with the result that (55a) and (55b) determine distinct (but partially overlapping) sets of focus-presupposition relations. Assuming that the intonation center of these sentences comes on the final constituent, Chicago, then there are several focus-presupposition possibilities determined according to principle (48). In both (55a) and (55b) the entire sentence may be the focus, or the VP may be the focus, and this is reflected in the fact that both may answer the following questions:

(56) a. What happened?

    b. What did he do?

However, note that the phrase a girl who he had met in Chicago forms a surface constituent in (55a), but not in (55b). (48) predicts that this can form a possible focus of (55a) but not of (55b), and this is borne out by noting the difference in naturalness these sentences manifest as responses to (57a):

(57) a. Who did he call up?

(57) b. He called up a girl who he had met in Chicago.

    c. #He called a girl up who he had met in Chicago.

(The symbol [#] is used to mark sentences which are judged as less natural responses). Sentence (57c) is judged to be less natural a response to (57a) than (57b) is. If we again use the paraphrase forms of the sort introduced above, we see why this is so:

(58) a. He called up someone -- who?

    b. He called up someone, namely, a girl who he had

       met in Chicago.

The presupposition "He called up someone" is shared by (57a) and (57b), however in (57c) the constituent structure is such that this presupposition cannot be formed according to principle (48). Thus, we predict that (57c) is a less natural response than (57b).[11] Differences in constituent structure allow one transformational variant to determine focus-presupposition relations that another variant does not. On the other hand, note that there is a sense in which differences in constituent structure do not have bearing on focus-presupposition relations. Consider the case in which the VP constituents of (55) are chosen as foci:

(59) a. called up a girl who he had met in Chicago

    b. called a girl up who he had met in Chicago

Even though the phrases chosen as foci are syntactically distinct, they determine the same focus in each case, since they are associated with the same portion of the semantic reading (i.e. are synonymous). In a similar fashion, consider pairs of clefted sentences such as:

(60) a. It was a girl from CHICAGO that he called up.

b. (The one) who he called up was a girl from CHICAGO.

Assuming that CHICAGO is the focus, the presupposition is determined by replacing that constituent with a variable. Using the symbol x for the variable, this would give us the following:

(61) a. [It was a girl from x that he called up]

b. [Who he called up was a girl from x]

Even though (61a) and (61b) are formed from syntactically distinct forms, they don't form distinct presuppositions, since they have identical readings. Hence, differences in constituent structure do not have any effect on focus-presupposition relations just as long as the syntactically distinct phrases are associated with just the same semantic representation.

It should be pointed out that any theory must have available to it the mechanisms for determining the semantic reading associated with given surface structure constituents. If the focus is determined by factors of the surface structure, then a theory, whether it is interpretive or not, must have some mechanism available to locate the semantic reading associated with some given chunk of the surface structure. Ray Jackendoff has suggested [personal communication] that a possible mechanism might be the use of 'identification indices' which could be associated with all nodes of the deep structure, and which would serve to track given nodes through a derivation. These would have no semantic content whatever, and would serve only to allow surface nodes to be traced through a derivation to determine what portions of the semantic reading are associated with these nodes.[12]

A clear implication of the data we have discussed so far is that derived phrases, not present at the deep structure level, can serve as foci. For example, note the following pairings:

(62) a. What is John like?

    b. John is <u>easy to please</u>.

    c. #It is easy to please John.

    d. #To please John is easy.

(63) a. John is <u>bound to lose</u>, isn't he?

    b. No, John is <u>certain to win</u>.

    c. #No, that John will win is certain.

    d. #No, it is certain that John will win.

(64) a. Were the Cambodians <u>invaded by the Viet Cong</u>?

   b. No, they were <u>attacked by the Americans</u>.

   c. #No, the Americans attacked them.

In each case a surface constituent of the question is paired
with a surface constituent of an answer. It is interesting
to note that paraphrases of these answers are judged to be
relatively less natural as responses. If we examine the focus-
presupposition relations involved, we see that the particular
constituent structures of the (b) sentences above allow certain foci to be formed which cannot be formed in the (c) and
(d) sentences because of their particular surface constituent
structures. Thus, the (b) sentences form more natural pairings with the (a) sentences than either the (c) or (d) sentences.

   We have discussed so far one area in which the notions
of focus and presupposition have linguistic significance,
using examples of the sort discussed in Chomsky [1969]. Insofar as these notions allow us to state what constitutes a
'natural response', they deserve to be included in the semantic representation of sentences. However, there is stronger
evidence for inclusion of focus in semantic representation,
from an area which is much less subject to dialectal variation. We refer here to the phenomenon of 'logical scope'.

5.1.2. Scope of Logical Elements. The notion of 'logical scope', which has been discussed primarily by Jackendoff [1969], refers to that aspect of the semantic interpretation of negation, questioning, and adverbial elements which has to do with the demarcation of that portion of a sentence which is taken to be modified by these items. The particular portion of a sentence which forms the domain of modification of these elements forms the 'scope' of such elements. We will discuss here the adverbial item even, and the principles which determine its scope, as a typical example of the nature of scope phenomena. Specifically, we will review recent work by S.R. Anderson [forthcoming, a] dealing with even.

Anderson begins with the fact (noted in Fischer [1968]) that the scope of even is associated with a constituent which has the intonation center:

(65) a. John even eats Skrunkies for DINNER.

b. John eats Skrunkies even for DINNER.

c. John even eats SKRUNKIES for dinner.

If the position of the intonation center is invariant, no semantic difference results from moving even to various positions in the sentence (within limitations noted by Anderson), as illustrated by (65a) and (65b), where the scope of even is the same in both cases. However, if the intonation center is shifted, then the scope of even is also changed, and shifts with the intonation center (compare (65a) and (65c)). This fact alone does not argue that the scope of even (i.e. the focus of the sentence) must be determined in surface structure. Indeed, Fischer [1968] argues that a feature [+Prominent] can be associated with any deep structure constituent, and that this feature will be realized phonetically as emphatic stress, and semantically as being a marker for constituents which form the scope of even. Such a feature would allow the interpretation of the scope of even to be carried out at the deep structure level, and this analysis would posit a transformation which would optionally move even (after it has been interpreted) to various positions in the sentence.

Anderson argues against this proposal by showing that (a) there are cases where the scope of even is not a single constituent, (b) where the scope of even is a constituent present only at the surface structure level, and (c) instances where an even-movement rule would have to violate general constraints on movement transformations. (Note that his arguments hold for a wide range of adverbials, as well, including only, just, also, as well as cases discussed in Jackendoff [1969]).

As an example of the first sort, Anderson gives the

following three sentences, along with their interpretations,
which we quote here:

(66) a. Jones can't even sell WHISKEY to the Indians.
(This implies that one can normally sell anything to the Indians: that is, that the Indians
are soft touches.)

b. Jones can't even sell whiskey to the INDIANS.
(This implies that normally one can sell whiskey
to anyone: that is, the whiskey is in great
demand.)

c. (Jones claims that he can sell refrigerators to
the Eskimos, but in fact) he can't even sell
WHISKEY to the INDIANS.
(This implies that of all the selling tasks one
could undertake, selling whiskey to the Indians
would be the easiest. This could be so either
because of a tremendous demand for whiskey, or
because the Indians are suckers. In fact, it
could be true for reasons distinct from both of
these: it might be that the government subsi-
dizes whiskey sales on the reservation, an advantage to local whiskey traders which is exten-
dable neither to other sales to Indians, nor to
whiskey sales elsewhere.)

The crucial point of these examples, as Anderson points out, comes in the interpretation of (66c), which could not be derived in deep structure by associating _even_ with either _whiskey_ or _Indians_. Furthermore, the interpretation of (66c) could not be derived by attaching _even_ to _both whiskey_ and _Indians_. This is the case since (66c) is not synonymous with either (66a) or (66b), and furthermore, there are no sentences such as the following from which (66c) could derive:

(67) *He can't sell even whiskey to even the Indians.

In other words, the special interpretation of (66c) is based on _one_ occurrence of _even_, the scope of which consists of _two_ separate stressed constituents. Since the two stressed constituents do not form a single larger constituent, (i.e. _whiskey to the Indians_ is not a constituent) it is impossible for the deep structure theory to associate _one_ occurrence of _even_ with _both_ of the stressed constituents. This, however, is just what needs to be done. If, on the other hand, we specify that the scope of _even_ is the focus constituent of a sentence, and further, if we allow for more than one focus per sentence, then the scope of _even_ will be assigned as the two constituents _whiskey_ and _Indians_.[13]

The second set of examples which Anderson brings up demonstrates that the scope of _even_ can be a constituent which is not present at the level of deep structure:

(68) Our new boss is a dream; he's pleasant, doesn't make
you work very hard, and he's even easy to get a
raise out of.

(69) Naked Came the Stranger was printed by a respectable
publisher, it was carried by all the big bookstores,
and it was even reviewed seriously by the New York
Times.

In (68) the scope of even is the phrase easy to get a raise
out of, and in (69) it is the phrase reviewed seriously by
the NYT. For reasons which have become familiar, neither
phrase is present at the level of deep structure. To take
one example, the constituent which forms the scope of even
in (69) is not present until after the application of the
passive rule. Anderson points out that it would be no solution to maintain that sentences which undergo the passive
rule are marked as such in deep structure, and thus that the
scope of even could somehow be determined at that level.
Such a move would mean that some principle would have to be
formulated to the effect that if the rule of passive is to
apply, the scope of even (when attached to the VP) consists
of the verb, and the subject of the sentence, and specifically
excludes the object. In other words, any alternative of this
sort simply builds in a semantic repetition of the syntactic
rule of passive in order to account for the scope of even at

the deep structure level.

Thus, just as phrases of the easy to please sort and phrases formed by the passive can form responses to question words (cf. (62)-(64)), they can also form the scope of adverbial elements such as even. Notice that if the scope of even can be a surface constituent, then we would expect to find other cases where optional movement transformations have affected constituent structure and thereby affected the focus-presupposition relations. This is just the case, in fact, as sentences such as the following show:

(70) Men who don't care for her will even date her.

(71) Men will even date her who don't care for her.

Let us assume that sentences (70) and (71) contain no instances of emphatic stress, but receive normal sentence stress patterns. This means that the intonation center of (70) falls on the constituent date, and in (71) falls on the constituent care (for). This is a result of the fact that if no emphatic stress is placed in these sentences, then the normal sentence intonation center will fall on the last major constituent (hence date and care). Note, now, that the two sentences receive quite different interpretations. (70) could be used in the following context:

(72) Men who don't care for her will do many things to make her angry -- they will even date her.

On the other hand, (71) would be used in a context such as:

> (73) She is so beautiful that many men will date her --
>
> even men who don't care for her.

In other words, (71) is synonymous with (74) and the marginal (75):

> (74) Even men who don't CARE for her will date her.

> (75) Men who don't CARE for her will even date her.

The point here is plain: the difference in meaning between (70) and (71) is brought about by the application of the optional rule of Relative Clause Extraposition, which maps (70) onto (71).[14] Since the effect of this rule is to add additional syntactic material to the end of the sentence, the normal intonation center therefore also shifts, given that normal sentence stress rules place the intonation center on the last major constituent. Since the intonation center shifts back in (71), the scope of _even_ changes accordingly and thus the difference in meaning between (70) and (71). Sentences such as (74) and (75) are synonymous with (71), since they have the intonation center on the same constituent as that in (71). Here, then, is another case which illustrates the impossibility of assigning the scope of _even_ as a deep structure constituent, for the simple reason that movement rules which apply optionally in the course of a derivation can significantly alter the ultimate surface constituent structure, and hence the focus-presupposition possibilities. Rather, the relevant generalizations concerning the scope of even are generalizations on surface syntactic structure, including facts of the phonetic contour. Such cases provide evidence that the scope of even (the focus of the sentence) is determined at the surface structure level.

A third set of arguments which Anderson uses to disprove a deep structure hypothesis involves the claim that an even-movement rule would necessarily violate general constraints on movement rules. Assume again that even is to be generated in deep structure, attached to the constituent which forms its scope, and assume for the sake of argument that it is possible to determine the scope of even at the deep structure level. Then assume that a transformation is posited which moves elements such as even to various positions in a sentence. Even if we accept this so far, Anderson shows that such a theory still fails, since the movement rule in question would have to move even out of complex NPs, a type of movement which is prohibited (cf. Ross [1967]). For example, Anderson gives the following cases:

    (76) a. You can do lots of things with bananas: I even
           know a guy who SMOKES them.

(76) b. (I gave many easy problems on the test --) I

even included a problem that FRESHMEN could solve.

In both cases the scope of even is understood to be the focus

of the sentence in question (i.e. scope = SMOKES in (76a),

and FRESHMEN in (76b)). Note that if even is to be associated

with its scope in deep structure, and then later moved by a

syntactic transformation, then such a transformation neces-

sarily violates movement constraints since in both (76a) and

(76b) even would have to be moved out of a relative clause.

Similar considerations hold for complex NPs with complement

structures, as Anderson's examples show:

(77) a. John even has the idea that HE is tall for a

Watusi.

b. John even has the idea that he is tall for a

WATUSI.

In these two sentences, the scope of even is interpreted as

the constituent with the intonation center, that is, even is

interpreted in the same way that it is in sentences such as:

(78) a. John has the idea that even HE is tall for a

Watusi.

b. John has the idea that he is tall even for a

WATUSI. [15]

Once again, if even were generated on the constituent which

forms its scope, and then transformationally moved, such a transformation would violate Ross's Complex NP Constraint (Ross [1967]). There is no need for such violation, however, since the scope of even can be determined in a straightforward manner in terms of factors of surface structure, i.e. focus.

Anderson thus argues against a theory which would associate even with its scope constituent in deep structure by demonstrating that in some cases there can be no one constituent which forms the scope of even, that in other cases there is no deep constituent which can be associated with even as its scope, and finally that an even-movement rule would necessarily violate general constraints on movement rules. As an alternative, Anderson advances a theory along lines proposed by Chomsky [1969] and Jackendoff [1969], namely, one in which the focus of a sentence is determined at the level of surface structure, and further that the scope of even is identified with the focus. (Certain limitations on the scope of even are noted by Anderson, but need not concern us here since they do not affect the main point.) Within this sort of framework, one can account for examples such as (68) and (69), and one avoids the problems connected with a deep structure theory of even. We will discuss the representation of sentences with even in section 6.1.2.

To sum up what we have said about focus and presupposition in these last few sections, we have tried to establish the following points:

(79) a. The <u>focus</u> is that portion of the semantic reading which is marked as prominent, in the sense that it represents 'novel' information (cf. (47)).

b. Focus-presupposition relations deserve to be part of the semantic reading of a sentence, in that these are crucial in explicating the structure of discourse, as well as logical scope.

c. The focus of a sentence is determined according to generalizations of (phonetically interpreted) surface structures.

In order to discuss focus in more detail, we must turn to the matter of semantic representation for focus.

6. The Semantic Notation for Focus and Presupposition

We have argued that in a question-answer pair such as the following:

(80) a. Who urged Nixon to appoint Carswell?

(80) b. MITCHELL urged Nixon to appoint Carswell.

an answer such as (80b) is a 'natural response' to a question

such as (80a). We arrive at this on the theory that the pre-

suppositions of the question and answer are identical, and

further that the focus of the answer specifies the variable

in the question. Conversely, we argue that a sentence such

as (81) does not answer (80a):

(81) Mitchell urged NIXON to appoint Carswell.

since their presuppositions do not match. Rather, (81)

answers a question such as (82):

(82) Who did Mitchell urge to appoint Carswell?

Surface structures are unfortunately not divided up

neatly into presuppositions and assertions, variables and

their specifications, and so on, and therefore we must con-

struct a semantic representation which will express clearly

and explicitly the focus-presupposition relations of sentences.

In particular such a semantic notation must allow straight-

forward comparison of questions and answers, in order to deter-

mine which pairings are "natural pairings"; further, the no-

tation must allow us to state semantic generalizations of

scope. We have already noted certain ways in which pairs such

as (80) can be paraphrased, in a manner which is highly sug-

gestive of a correct semantic representation. Consider the

following paraphrase forms for the sentences of (80):

(83) a. Someone urged Nixon to appoint Carswell -- who?

b. Someone urged Nixon to appoint Carswell, namely,
MITCHELL.

When sentences such as those of (80) are put into a form such as (83), the focus-presupposition relations are revealed, and cast in the form of (83) we can compare question-answer pairs such as (80) in a straightforward manner to determine whether presuppositions match, and so forth. Similarly, (81) and (82) can be placed in this form:

(84) a. Mitchell urged someone to appoint Carswell --
who?

b. Mitchell urged someone to appoint Carswell,
namely, NIXON.

To see why (81) does not answer (80a), we compare paraphrase (83a) (for (80a)) and paraphrase (84b) (for (81)), and we note that the presuppositions of question and answer do not match:

(85) a. Someone urged Nixon to appoint Carswell -- who?

b. Mitchell urged someone to appoint Carswell,
namely, NIXON.

Since paraphrases such as (83) and (84) reveal the focus-presupposition structure of questions and answers, let us construct a semantic representation along these lines. In

particular, we propose to represent focus-presupposition relations in the following manner:

(86) a. [[x urged Nixon to appoint Carswell], [x = ?]]

b. [[x urged Nixon to appoint Carswell], [x =
Mitchell]]

(86) is the representation of the sentences of (80), and for
the sentences (81) and (82) we have similar representations:

(87) a. [[Mitchell urged x to appoint Carswell], [x =
Nixon]]

b. [[Mitchell urged x to appoint Carswell], [x =
?]]^{16}

The expressions given in (86) and (87) represent the partitioning of the semantic reading into a focal portion and
presupposed portion. For every focus-presupposition relation
which a given sentence has, there is an expression such as
the ones above. Such representations are formed as follows.
The interpretive principle for focus chooses a constituent of
the surface syntactic structure which contains the intonation
center. It locates that portion of the semantic reading of
the sentence which is associated with this particular surface
constituent. Once this portion of the reading has been located, then expressions such as those of (86) and (87) can be
formed automatically: the focal portion of the reading is

replaced with a variable, forming the presupposition (represented as the leftmost bracketed expression); the rightmost bracketed expression is formed by linking the variable of the presupposition and the focal material with the specification operator [=]. (In some cases, as we will see, the link between variable and focal material is the predicational operator [is]).

The presupposition is formally separated from the focus expression by the symbol [,], which we employ here as an ad-hoc device to represent the relation between presupposition and focus. The use of an ad-hoc device reflects the fact that at the current stage of research it is not clear how presuppositions are to be formally related to other portions of a semantic reading, i.e. what sort of logical connective(s) should be employed. Insofar as we can bring relevant evidence to bear on the issue, however, it seems that we can say that conjunction (i.e. logical conjunction with and) is not the proper device to relate given expressions with their presuppositions. One reason has to do with certain philosophical problems which relate to assignment of truth values. If assertions and presuppositions are related by conjunction, then falsity of any one conjunct entails falsity of the entire conjunction (which we assume to be a property of logical conjunction in general). Consider, for example, sentences such as:

> (88) a. MITCHELL urged Strom Thurmond to appoint Carswell.
>
> b. It was MITCHELL who urged Strom Thurmond to appoint Carswell.

On the conjunction hypothesis, this would be represented as:

> (89) [[x̲ urged Strom Thurmond to appoint Carswell] and
>
> [x̲ = Mitchell]]

Suppose thatthe leftmost expression of (89) were false, i.e. that Thurmond has not been urged to appoint Carswell. Since (89) is a conjunction, and one of its conjuncts is false, then the entire conjunction is also false. Insofar as intuitive judgements can be brought to bear on such issues, it seems that the conjunction theory makes false predictions in this case. For example, consider a discourse such as:

> (90) a. Someone urged the President to appoint Carswell, but I don't know who.
>
> b. In fact, it was MITCHELL who urged Strom Thurmond to appoint Carswell.

Confronted with a response such as (90b), it would be odd to say that it is _false_. While it is the case that the speaker who utters (90b) has failed to make a true assertaion, it would be more accurate to say that it is irrelevant to speak

of truth or falsity for sentences such as (90b). The speaker
who utters (90b) makes the false assumption that Strom
Thurmond is the President. In response to a speaker who
utters (90b) we might say, "You are mistaken in your assumptions about who is President", but it would be rather strange
to say, "What you just said is false".[17] In other words, the
logical relation between presupposition and assertion is such
that falsity of the presupposition does not entail falsity of
the entire expression. If this is the case, then conjunction
is not the proper device to connect presupposition and assertion.

Another reason why the use of conjunction seems to be
mistaken concerns the representation of questions, such as
(86a) and (87b). That is, logical conjunctions of non-inter-
rogative statements with interrogative statements are anomalous. If such conjunctions are possible, then it should be
possible to have sentences such as:

    (91) *Someone urged Nixon to appoint Carswell, and who

           urged Nixon to appoint Carswell?

We assume that in general such conjunctions are not permitted,
but this would be just what is required in the conjunction
theory. That is, representations such as (86a) would be in
the following form:

(92) [[x urged Nixon to appoint Carswell] and [x = ?]]

A logical conjunction such as (92) is excluded on general grounds, and thus the use of conjunction is inappropriate.

For reasons such as these, it is wisest to leave open the question of what sort of logical connective is used to represent the relation of given expressions to their presuppositions. We know that the relation is such that falsity of the presupposition should not entail falsity of the entire representation, and further that the logical connection permits non-interrogatives to be connected with interrogatives. These properties are not properties of a conjunction relation. At worst, semantic theory must posit a primitive relation of presupposition, which is taken as unanalyzable and universally defined. At any rate, we leave open this question, and use the device [,] in our representations.

Before discussing the justification for the proposed semantic notation, we should discuss here an important aspect of the way focus is represented in this notation. That is, note that the focus of a sentence, in this notation, is not just a constituent of the sentence, but rather it is a semantic proposition which contains a specification relation between a variable and some constituent. Consider a typical example:

(93) a. Mozart wrote 4 piano QUARTETS.

      b. [[Mozart wrote 4 x], [x = piano quartets]]

The rightmost expression is the representation of focus, and
thus the focus in semantic representation is a specification
relation, and it is not merely a constituent isolated from
the rest of the sentence. We shall examine the reasons for
this in a moment. The term 'focus' is thus ambiguous. When
we use the term 'focus' (or 'focus constituent') with regard
to surface syntactic structures it refers to a surface constituent which contains the intonation center. However, when
the term is used in regard to semantic representations, it
refers to the semantic proposition which specifies a variable.[18]

6.1. Justification of the Proposed Semantic Notation. In
this section we shall discuss in greater detail the proposed
semantic notation, and we will justify this particular notation on several grounds. First, we show that from the stand-
point of the general interpretation of focus, the proposed
notation captures what is meant when we say that the focus of
a sentence represents 'novel' information. Secondly, we show
that the notation allows us to relate semantically a wide

range of diverse syntactic forms. It allows us to state clearly the semantic parallels between WH-questions, yes/no questions, and declarative sentences of both clefted and non-
clefted sorts. Finally, we show that the notation proposed
provides just the sort of representation needed to account
for so-called "attraction to focus" phenomena in the area of
logical scope.

6.1.1. Focus as 'Novel' Information. We have stated

that the focus constituent of a sentence is interpreted as
representing novel information (within some universe of discourse). To phrase the matter in this way, however, is misleading, since it implies that what is interpreted as novel
is the lexical material which makes up the focus constituent.
It is clear, however, that this is not the correct formulation. Consider a sentence such as the following:

(96) Nixon conferred with LAIRD on the Cambodian question.
Let us suppose that the focus is the constituent LAIRD. It
would be misleading to say that this constituent is novel,
i.e. that the lexical and semantic information associated
with this constituent is novel. The simplest counterexample

is the case in which two speakers have been discussing Nixon, Laird, Mitchell, and so on, in a conversation in which each of these persons has been mentioned repeatedly. If sentence (96) is put in such a context, then there is nothing at all novel about the <u>constituent</u> LAIRD and the semantic information it contains. We recall here Halliday's statement (cf. (47)) that what is focal is novel, <u>not</u> in the sense that it cannot have been mentioned, but in the sense that it is presented as being 'non-recoverable'. Even if the constituent LAIRD has been previously mentioned, it is still interpreted as representing novel information in some sense. When we examine in what sense we mean the term 'novel', we note that the novelty associated with the constituent LAIRD in (96) is the novelty associated with the <u>identification</u> of Laird as the one who Nixon conferred with. In other words, it is not the constituent <u>Laird</u> which is novel, it is the particular <u>seman-tic relation</u> in which this constituent participates that is novel. If we examine the semantic representation which this sentence would have in our proposed notation, we see that the representation of focus in this notation is in fact a propo-sition expressing a semantic relation:

(97) [[Nixon conferred with <u>x</u> on the Cambodian question],

[<u>x</u> = Laird]]

Given that we take the constituent LAIRD in (96) to be the focus, the interpretive principle marks off the portion of the reading associated with this constituent. Once this portion is marked off, a representation such as (97) is formed. Given this sort of representation we can state quite precisely just what aspect of the reading is interpreted as novel information. We simply state that the rightmost bracketed expression, as a whole, is interpreted as novel information in the semantic reading. This captures quite accurately the fact that the lexical material associated with the focus is not interpreted as novel, but rather that the particular semantic relation in which the focus constituent participates is interpreted as novel. This aspect of the proposed representation will become even more important when discussing the matter of scope and attraction to focus.

6.1.2. Logical Scope and Attraction to Focus. We have discussed the adverbial element even and we have seen that its scope is associated with a surface constituent which contains the intonation center, i.e. a possible focus of the sentence in which even occurs. We will consider now further examples

of what Jackendoff [1969] has termed 'attraction to focus',
in order to see how attraction phenomena are represented in
the notation we propose.

Consider first yes/no questions, such as the following
set:

(98) a. Did NIXON confer with Mitchell on the Cambodian
question?

b. Did Nixon CONFER with Mitchell on the Cambodian
question?

c. Did Nixon confer with MITCHELL on the Cambodian
question?

Even though each sentence is in the form of a question, it is
clear that what is under question in each case is only a portion of the sentence, not the entire sentence. As we see
from the questions in (98), the portion understood to be in
question is just the constituent which contains the intonation
center, and for this reason we can say that questioning in
these cases 'attracts' to the focus constituent.

The question now arises as to how to represent the fact
that the scope of questioning in these cases consists of the
focus constituent. What does it mean to say that questioning
is limited to just one constituent of a sentence? Semantically, questions are formed from propositions, not from single

constituents. However, given the notation we propose, it is possible to state the facts concerning scope of questioning in a natural manner, precisely because the focus is represented as a proposition. Thus, the questions of (98) would be represented as:

(99) a. [[$\underline{x}$ conferred with Mitchell on the Cambodian question], [[$\underline{x}$ = Nixon] ?]]

b. [[Nixon did $\underline{x}$ with Mitchell on the Cambodian question], [[$\underline{x}$ = confer] ?]][19]

c. [[Nixon conferred with $\underline{x}$ on the Cambodian question], [[$\underline{x}$ = Mitchell] ?]]

We can make the notion of attraction to focus precise in this case, by stating that the question operator is to be associated with the rightmost expression. Since this expression is in fact a proposition, there is no semantic problem about associating the question operator with just a constituent of the sentence. Furthermore, such representations correctly indicate that the questions of (98) are all questions of identity. WH-questions are also questions of identity; however, instead of requesting confirmation of a given identity (as in (98)), such questions request complete specification for the variable of the presupposition. In order to represent this difference, and the regularize the notation we are using, we represent

WH-questions as follows:

(100) a. Who did Nixon confer with on the Cambodian
question?

b. [[Nixon conferred with $\underline{x}$ on the Cambodian
question], [[$\underline{x}$ = Δ] ?]]

An expression such as [[$\underline{x}$ = Δ] ?] represents a request for
specification of the variable, while an expression such as
[[$\underline{x}$ = Mitchell] ?] represents a request for confirmation
of the given specification.

If we sum up what we have said so far, we note that the
sentences in (101) receive the representations of (102):

(101) a. Who did Nixon confer with on the Cambodian
question?

b. Did Nixon confer with MITCHELL on the Cambodian
question?

c. Was it MITCHELL·that Nixon conferred with on
the Cambodian question?

d. Was the one who Nixon conferred with on the
Cambodian question MITCHELL?

e. Nixon conferred with MITCHELL on the Cambodian
question.

f. It was MITCHELL that Nixon conferred with on
the Cambodian question.

(101) g. The one who Nixon conferred with on the
Cambodian question was MITCHELL.

(102) a. [[Nixon conferred with x on the Cambodian
question], [[x = Δ] ?]]

b. [[Nixon conferred with x on the Cambodian
question], [[x = Mitchell] ?]]

c. [[Nixon conferred with x on the Cambodian
question], [[x = Mitchell]]]

(101a) is represented as (102a), (101b-(101d) are represented
as (102b), and (101e)-(101g) are represented as (102c). The
significant point here is that the notation allows us to capture the semantic parallels holding among a wide range of
syntactic forms. By inspection of the leftmost bracketed
expression we can sort sentences into natural semantic
classes (i.e. sets of presupposition-sharing sentences). We
can cite precisely how they are similar, and, by inspection
of the rightmost bracketed expression, we can cite just how
they differ.

If we examine now examples of logical scope of negation,
we see that arguments analogous to those involving scope of
questioning can be made for the notation we propose. Once
again, the significant feature of our analysis is that the
focus is represented as a semantic proposition. Consider,

then, sentences such as the following:

(103) a. The NAVY doesn't want new bombers.

b. The Navy doesn't want NEW bombers.

c. The Navy doesn't want new BOMBERS.

Each of the sentences of (103) contains a negative, and in each case the scope of the negative is taken to be only a portion of the sentence. The particular portion which forms the scope of the negative must in fact be a constituent which is a possible focus constituent of the sentence. Hence in (103a) it is not denied that some organization wants new bombers, it is only denied that this organization is the Navy; in (103b) it is not denied that the Navy wants bombers, it is only denied that it wants _new_ bombers; finally, in (103c) it is not denied that the Navy wants something new, it is only denied that the Navy wants bombers which are new. In each case the scope of the negation is the focus constituent. This phenomenon is quite general, and is not limited to sentences in which the negative particle _not_ appears. The same attraction to focus occurs when the negative is incorporated into a given morpheme, as well as when the negative occurs in such phrases as _it is not the case that_. Furthermore, the same phenomenon occurs with inherently negative verbs such as _deny_ and _doubt_. Consider, for example:

(104) a. Nixon said nothing about AMERICAN sanctuaries.

b. Nixon said nothing about American SANCTUARIES.

(105) a. It is not the case that the NAVY wants bombers.

b. It is not the case that the Navy wants BOMBERS.

(106) a. I $\left\{ \begin{array}{l} \text{doubt} \\ \text{deny} \end{array} \right\}$ that the SENATE will back Nixon.

b. I $\left\{ \begin{array}{l} \text{doubt} \\ \text{deny} \end{array} \right\}$ that the Senate will back NIXON.

In (104a) the negation contained in the morpheme nothing is attracted to the focus constituent. The sentence presupposes that Nixon said something about some sanctuaries, and the denial is only that he spoke about American sanctuaries. Similar considerations hold for (104b) and the sentences of (105). In (106) the scope of doubt or denial is governed as well by attraction to focus. Thus, in (106a) there is a presupposition that someone or something will back Nixon, and the doubt is limited to the identification of the Senate as that which will back him.

Once again, we ask what it means to say that negation is attracted to the focus constituent. Once again the answer is that negation is not associated with a constituent, but rather is associated with the proposition which represents the focus in the reading of the sentence. This results in representations such as the following for the sentences of (103):

(107) a. [[The $\underline{x}$ wants new bombers next year],

[NEG [$\underline{x}$ = the Navy]]]

b. [[The Navy wants bombers which are $\underline{x}$]

[NEG [$\underline{x}$ = new]]]

c. [[The Navy wants new $\underline{x}$], [NEG [$\underline{x}$ = bombers]]]

On the same principle, the sentences of (104)-(106) receive the following representations (in respective order):

(108) a. [[Nixon said something about $\underline{x}$ sanctuaries],

[NEG [$\underline{x}$ = American]]]

b. [[Nixon said something about American $\underline{x}$],

[NEG [$\underline{x}$ = sanctuaries]]]

(109) a. [[The $\underline{x}$ wants bombers], [NEG [$\underline{x}$ = the Navy]]]

b. [[The Navy wants $\underline{x}$], [NEG [$\underline{x}$ = bombers]]]

(110) a. [[$\underline{x}$ will back Nixon], [I $\left\{\begin{array}{l}\text{doubt} \\ \text{deny}\end{array}\right\}$ [$\underline{x}$ = the Senate]]]

b. [[The Senate will back $\underline{x}$], [I $\left\{\begin{array}{l}\text{doubt} \\ \text{deny}\end{array}\right\}$ [$\underline{x}$ = Nixon]]]

The proposed notation thus allows us to isolate precisely the portions of the sentences which come under negation.

If we consider now other elements which have logical scope, it is possible to show that the notation proposed for focus and presupposition allows us to state generalizations over a wide range of cases. Returning to a consideration of the adverbial particle _even_, we have already noted that _even_ takes as its scope the focus of a sentence:

(111) a. The Air Force even wants to spray Cambodian VILLAGES.

b. The Air Force even wants to spray CAMBODIAN villages.

c. The Air Force even wants to SPRAY Cambodian villages.

d. The Air Force even WANTS to spray Cambodian villages.

Ignoring the placement of _even_ for a moment, we represent the focus-presupposition relations of (111) as follows:

(112) a. [[The Air Force wants to spray Cambodian x], [x = villages]]

b. [[The Air Force wants to spray x villages], [x = Cambodian]]

c. [[The Air Force wants [the Air Force x Cambodian villages], [x = spray]]

d. [[The Air Force x [the Air Force spray Cambodian villages], [x = want]][20]

We have talked about the scope of _even_ so far, however,

we must examine a little further what even means and what it
means to say that some item forms the scope of even. Following Bruce Fraser [1969], we can say that a sentence with even
such as (111a) has at least the following isolable parts in
its interpretation (cf. Fraser [1969, II-3]):

> (113) a. The Air Force wants to spray Cambodian villages.
>
> b. The Air Force wants to spray other Cambodian
> things.
>
> c. The speaker would not expect (and would not ex-
> pect the hearer to expect) that villages would
> be one of the desired targets of the Air Force
> spraying campaign.

Of these portions of the interpretation of (111a), (113a) represents that semantic information read from the deep structure, i.e. grammatical relations. The semantic contribution
of even is found in (113b) and (113c). Leaving aside (113b)
for the moment, we note that (113c) is the central aspect of
the interpretation of even. The presence of even in a sentence such as (111a) indicates that the speaker judges as
unexpected (or, assumes that the hearer will judge as unexpected) the fact that villages are desired targets. Such a
speaker might assume that Cambodian jungles or Cambodian
military installations are appropriate targets for spraying,

but it is unexpected that civilian villages are targets. In
other words, the assertion of specification in representations
such as (112a) is precisely that portion of the reading which
represents that information which is taken to be unexpected.

Once again, scope is taken to be the proposition which
represents the focus. If even contains as part of its meaning a predicate unexpected, then what we mean when we say that
the scope of even attracts to focus is that this predicate
of unexpectedness is predicated of the focus expression:

(114) [[The Air Force wants to spray Cambodian x],

[[x = villages] UNEXPECTED]]

Whether or not this is viewed as the correct way to represent
the meaning of even, the point to be made here is that the
semantic effect of even is limited to the rightmost bracketed
expression.

At this point we ask whether there are further aspects
of the interpretation of even which must also appear in representations such as (114). In particular, does (113b) appear
explicitly in the semantic representation of sentences containing even? (113b) represents that aspect of the interpretation of even which we can label the implication of non-
uniqueness: to say that the Air Force even wants to spray
villages is to imply that villages are not the only thing

the Air Force wishes to spray, that there are other things
the Air Force wants to spray.

With respect to this aspect of the interpretation of
even, Fraser [1969, Il-4] states:

> The effect of even on the [item which forms its
> scope] permits the hearer to make the inference
> that the referent of [the scope item] must be
> viewed as a member of a set of similar tokens with
> which it (the referent) can be contrasted within
> the context of the remainder of the sentence.

Thus, Fraser's view is that the portion of the interpretation
of even represented in (113b) is to be regarded as an implication (in the sense of Austin [1962]). I feel that this
view is correct (i.e. (113b) does not appear explicitly in
the reading).

The evidence we can present here for this view is based
on the fact that it is impossible to determine what the analogue of (113b) would be. Consider, for example, a sentence
such as:

(115) The Air Force even WANTS to bomb peasants.

We can say that this sentence expresses the proposition that
the Air Force wants to bomb peasants, and that one would not
expect the Air Force to want to bomb peasants. However, what

is the analogue of (113b) for (115)? Perhaps we could say
that (115) implies that the Air Force has other <u>attitudes</u>
toward bombing peasants. This is reasonable since we can
have contrasts such as:

> (116) The Air Force not only <u>likes</u> to bomb peasants -- it
> even WANTS to bomb peasants.

However, if this were the only implication of (115), then we
would not expect to have contrasts such as:

> (117) The Air Force has not only been <u>ordered</u> to bomb
> peasants -- it even WANTS to bomb peasants.

In fact, as the following examples show, we cannot isolate
any single implication of sentence (115) as being part of its
reading, since many different kinds of contrasts are possible
with the verb WANT:

> (118) a. The Air Force not only <u>must</u> bomb peasants -- it
> even WANTS to bomb them.
>
> b. The Air Force not only <u>can</u> bomb peasants -- it
> even WANTS to bomb them.
>
> c. The immorality of the Vietnam War is quite clear.
> For example, not only does the Air Force <u>bomb</u>
> peasants, it even WANTS to bomb peasants.

In other words, the verb WANT can be contrasted in a great
number of ways, and it is impossible to isolate any single

implication of non-uniqueness as being the implication found
in the reading of sentences such as (115). For this reason
we maintain that the readings of sentences containing even do
not explicitly contain anything analogous to (113b), since
this implication of non-uniqueness cannot be uniquely determined.[21]

To sum up what we have discussed in this section, we have
attempted to justify the proposed semantic notation on the
grounds that it allows us to express certain semantic generalizations. It allows us to express the semantic relation
between questions, clefted sentences, and non-clefted sentences (cf. (101) and (102)). As a result of this property,
it allows us to define in a simple way such notions as
"natural response". Furthermore, by representing the focus
as a proposition in which a variable is specified, the notation allows us to state generalizations concerning logical
scope of negation, questioning and items such as even. The
general principle for scope which we have arrived at is the
following:

(119) The logical scope of negation, questioning, and
      adverbial items such as even is restricted to the
      proposition in the semantic reading which repre-
      sents the focus.

The proposed notation is justified insofar as it allows us to capture these generalizations.

6.2. Intonation and Semantic Representation.

In discussing the logical scope of negation and its semantic representation we concluded that the scope of negation is always located outside the expression which represents the presupposition, as stated in (119). However, this account leaves out a significant factor in interpreting such sentences, namely, the intonation contour. In fact, the semantic representation of such sentences changes significantly depending on various factors of tone contour.

6.2.1. Contradictive vs. Conclusive.

The examples of negation we have discussed so far are all examples in which the scope of negation is restricted to the focus constituent. Under certain conditions, however, the negation can be part of the presupposition, and this has to do with the intonation pattern of the sentence. In particular, the examples we have

been dealing with could be read with at least two distinct
intonation patterns, which we refer to as the contradictive
intonation pattern and the conclusive intonation pattern (the
term 'conclusive' is taken from Bolinger [1965, p. 313]).
The contradictive pattern can be illustrated in the following
context:

(120) Mitchell urged Nixon to appoint Carswell, didn't
he.

(121) No, MITCHELL didn't urge Nixon to appoint Carswell
(-- FINCH did).

(122) No, it wasn't MITCHELL who urged Nixon to appoint
Carswell (it was FINCH).

(123) No, the one who urged Nixon to appoint Carswell
wasn't MITCHELL (-- it was FINCH).

Sentences (120)-(123), excluding the parenthesized phrase,
have the contradictive intonation pattern. As the name implies, this pattern is typically used in contradicting or
correcting another speaker's statements. The primary characteristic of this intonation pattern is a rising tone pattern at the end of the sentence. Furthermore, the sentence-
long intonation contour is perceived to have a rising-falling-
rising pattern:

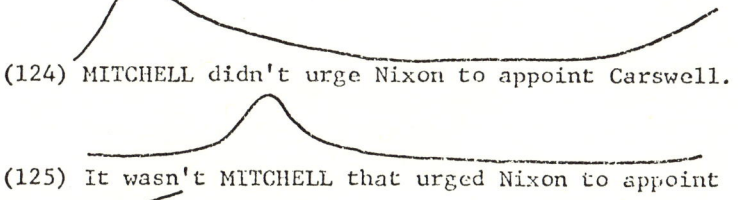

(124) MITCHELL didn't urge Nixon to appoint Carswell.

(125) It wasn't MITCHELL that urged Nixon to appoint
Carswell.[22]

The contours of sentences such as (124) and (125) are no
doubt more subtle; however, the rough pattern indicated is
enough to distinguish the significant features of the contradictive pattern from others. In our discussion of such patterns, we will represent rising tone at the end of a sentence
with an arrow [↗] placed at the end of the sentence; the
rising-falling-rising tone pattern will be indicated by the
symbol [∨] at the end of the sentence.

The conclusive intonation pattern, on the other hand,
can be illustrated in a context such as:

(126) Who was the one who didn't urge Nixon to appoint
Carswell?

(127) MITCHELL didn't urge Nixon to appoint Carswell.

(128) It was MITCHELL who didn't urge Nixon to appoint
Carswell.

(129) The one who didn't urge Nixon to appoint Carswell
was MITCHELL.

The conclusive intonation pattern, as the name implies, is

used at the end of an utterance, and indicates that the
speaker has finished with his discourse and has no further
information to add. The central difference between this
pattern and the contradictive pattern is that in the conclusive pattern the tone <u>falls</u> at the end of the sentence (falling tone at the end of the sentence will be indicated by the
use of the period [.]). Furthermore, the sentence-long intonation pattern of the conclusive pattern is perceived to be
level, (except, of course, on a constituent with emphatic
stress) and steadily drops:

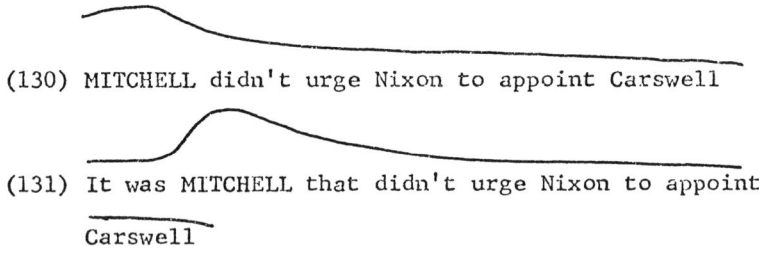

(130) MITCHELL didn't urge Nixon to appoint Carswell

(131) It was MITCHELL that didn't urge Nixon to appoint
Carswell

We will represent this tone pattern with the symbol [↘] at
the end of the sentence. If we re-examine the sentences (121)-
(123) we see that both contradictive and conclusive intonation patterns are present:

(132) It wasn't MITCHELL who urged Nixon to appoint
Carswell   [↗] -- It was FINCH who urged Nixon
to appoint Carswell. [↘]

Thus the patterns are differentiated on the basis of rising

tone vs. falling tone at the end of the sentence, as well as a contour of rising-falling-rising vs. a contour of level-falling. Even though these are rough properties, they are sufficient to distinguish the patterns.

Note now that the semantic interpretation of such sentences changes radically according to whether the sentence has a contradictive pattern or a conclusive pattern. This is especially true for non-clefted sentences such as (121) and (127) which are otherwise formally identical in surface structure. Specifically, the negation goes with the focus constituent when the sentence has a contradictive intonation pattern, but is part of the presupposition when the sentence has a conclusive intonation pattern. Thus, sentences (121)-(123) have the representation (133), and the sentences (127)-(129) have the representation (134):

(133) [[$\underline{x}$ urged Nixon to appoint Carswell], [[$\underline{x}$ = Mitchell] NEG]]

(134) [[$\underline{x}$ didn't urge Nixon to appoint Carswell], [$\underline{x}$ = Mitchell]]

The non-clefted sentences (121) and (127) receive two different interpretations strictly on the basis of the intonation patterns, since they are lexically and structurally identical. (Note also the fact that even though clefted sentences reflect this difference in interpretation formally -- that is, the negative can either appear on the copula or in the embedded clause -- the intonation patterns described above are still required. Sentences (122) and (123) must have the contradictive intonation pattern, and sentences (128) and (129) must have the conclusive pattern.)

Isolating the conclusive and contradictive intonation patterns has important consequences for the semantic interpretation of a wide range of sentences. These involve problems connected with the interaction of negation with adverbials, as well as interaction of negation with quantifiers. For example, consider the much-discussed ambiguity in sentences such as the following (discussed first by Lakoff [1965], and more recently by Jackendoff [1969] and Lasnik [1970]:

(135) John doesn't beat his wife because he lóves her. This can mean either that John does not beat his wife, the reason being that he loves her, or it can mean that John in fact does beat his wife, however, we cannot ascribe this habit to his loving her. In either sense the intonation center of the sentence is on the item loves, and further, there is no formal lexical or structural difference associated with the ambiguity. In fact, only the intonation pattern differentiates these senses. Consider (135) read with the

contradictive pattern and also the conclusive pattern:

(136) a. John doesn't beat his wife because he LOVES her. [↗]

b. John doesn't beat his wife because he LOVES her. [↘]

According to what we have stated above, in (136a), which has a contradictive pattern, the negation must be associated with the focus of the sentence. However, in (136b), with a conclusive pattern, the negation must be placed within the presupposition. This principle will give us the following representations (where (137a) represents (136a), and (137b) represents (136b)):

(137) a. [[John beats his wife because he $\underline{x}$ her],

[[$\underline{x}$ = love] NEG]]

b. [[John doesn't beat his wife because he $\underline{x}$ her],

[$\underline{x}$ = love]]

Let us note again that the clefted sentences corresponding to the two sentences of (136) also have the same intonation patterns:

(138) a. It is not because he LOVES her that John beats his wife

b. It is because he LOVES her that John doesn't beat his wife

These receive the same interpretation as the sentences of (136), namely, the representations of (137).

So far, we have discussed examples which contain the negative particle not; however, the same considerations hold for cases involving instances of constituent negation and adverbial clauses. For example, consider the following sentence (from Lasnik [1970]):

(139) No one grows cotton because of government subsidies

This can be read with either the contradictive or conclusive patterns, and would receive the following representations:

(140) a. [[People grow cotton because of x], [[x = government subsidies] NEG]] (╱ , [∿])

    b. [[People don't grow cottong because of x], [x = government subsidies]] (. , [↘])

As we have seen in previous examples, the negative, even though it is a part of a pro-form morpheme, still attracts to focus with contradictive intonation.

Analogous considerations hold when we examine the interaction of the scope of negation and quantification. The distinction between contradictive and conclusive intonation differentiates those readings in which the quantifier is understood to be within the scope of negation from those readings in which it is taken to be outside the scope of negation (cf.

Jackendoff [1969]). Consider, for example, sentences such as:

(141) a. ALL the boys don't want ice cream

b. MOST of the boys don't want ice cream

(142) ALL the boys don't read many books

(143) a. THE BOYS don't want all of the ice cream

b. THE BOYS don't want most of the ice cream

Each of the sentences listed above (with the intonation centers as indicated) can be read with either the contradictive
pattern or the conclusive pattern. Taking (141a), read with
a conclusive pattern, the quantifier is understood to be outside the scope of negation, and read with the contradictive
pattern the quantifier is understood to be within the scope
of negation. Consider:

(144) a. It's all the boys that don't want ice cream
[conclusive]

b. It's not all the boys that want ice cream
[contradictive]

The sentences of (141) will receive the following sorts of
representations following the principles we have discussed:

(145) a. [[$\underline{x}$ don't want ice cream], [$\underline{x}$ = all the boys]]
(., [↘])

b. [[$\underline{x}$ want ice cream], [NEG [$\underline{x}$ = all the boys]]]
(↗ , [↗])

(146) a. [[x don't want ice cream], [x = most of the

boys]] (., [↘])

b. [[x want ice cream], [NEG [x = most of the

boys]]] (↗ , [↗↘])

Thus, even though the quantifiers are to the left of the

negation in surfact structure, they may be interpreted as be-

ing within the scope of negation when the sentence is read

with the contradictive pattern. This happens when the quan-

tifiers are part of the focus phrase (or, alternatively, are

the foci themselves). Since negation attracts to focus with

this intonation pattern, the quantifier will automatically

come within the scope of negation within the system we pro-

pose (cf. (145b), and (146b)). However, when the sentence

is read with conclusive intonation, the negation remains as

part of the presupposition, and the focus phrase is removed,

thus removing the quantifier from the scope of negation (cf.

(145a) and (146a)).

Consider now (142). The interpretive system we have pro-

posed predicts that when the quantifier all is perceived as

being within the scope of negation, then the quantifier many

is taken to be outside the scope of negation, and vice-versa.

This is due to the fact that (142) receives the following

representations:

(147) a. [[x don't read many books], [x = all the boys]]

(., [↘])

b. [[x read many books], [NEG [x = all the boys]]]

(↗, [∨])

These interpretations can be made clearer by noting the cleft counterparts for (142):

(148) a. It's all the boys that don't read many books

[conclusive]

b. It's not all the boys that read many books

[contradictive]

Thus, the ambiguity of (142) is again a consequence of the different principles of interpretation associated with different intonation patterns.

Finally consider the sentences of (143). The quantifiers in these cases come within the scope of negation with the conclusive pattern, when the negation remains in the presupposition. The quantifier is not interpreted as being within the scope of negation when the sentence is read with a contradictive pattern, since the negation is attracted to the focus. The difference, again, can be paraphrased as follows:

(149) a. It's the boys who don't want all the ice cream

[conclusive]

249

(149) b. It's not the boys who want all the ice cream

[contradictive]

The representations for (143) (using only (143a) as an ex-

ample) would work out as follows:

(150) a. [[x don't want all the ice cream], [x = all

the boys]]

b. [[x want all the ice cream], [NEG [x = all the

boys]]]

From such examples, and examples discussed earlier, we
see that various factors of phonetically interpreted surface
structures play a role in marking off focus-presupposition
relations. The location of the intonation center is the
crucial factor in determining the focus constituent of a
sentence, and we see that intonation patterns play a significant role in the determination of scope of negation. These
facts argue that interpretive principles must be sensitive to
a variety of intonational phenomena (and not merely the location of the intonation center), since these, along with surface constituent structure, affect in a significant way how
various portions of a semantic reading are inter-related.

7. Concluding Remarks on Clefted Sentences

Given the sort of framework we have outlined above, we can see how it is possible that clefted sentences deriving from more than one source can be assigned only one reading. Consider again the following situation:

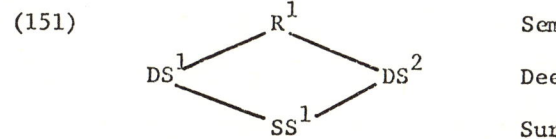

(151)   Semantic Reading

                                             Deep Structure

                                             Surface Structure

We have tried to show that in the sort of situation represented by (151) the two deep structure sources in question are semantically equivalent. Since these express the same semantic information, no ambiguity can arise from this level. Furthermore, we have attempted to demonstrate that the focus-presupposition relations are determined by factors of surface structures. If this is true, there are several consequences of relevance to the theory we have outlined.

First of all, the deep structure source containing the empty [Δ] need not have any indication as to which constituent is the focus constituent, since this will be determined at a point after the application of the extraction rule. Thus, the syntactically motivated deep structure posited by the extraction theory causes no semantic problems, and indeed,

given that focus-presupposition relations are not determined
by properties of deep structure phrase markers, it is not surprising to find that (at least a class of) deep phrase markers
provide no indication whatever of what the focus-presupposition relations are.

Secondly, and more directly related to (151), if focus-
presupposition relations are determined by factors of surface
structure, then SS^1 of (151) will be assigned only one set
of these relations, there being only a single surface structure. Thus, there can be no ambiguity arising with respect
to focus-presupposition relations. Since the deep structure
sources are equivalent, only one set of grammatical relations
are assigned, and since the focus-presupposition relations
are determined by factors of surface structure only one set
of such relations is assigned to one surface structure.

8. A Note on Syntactic Representation vs. Semantic Represen-
tation

The issues we have discussed above and in the last
several chapters have some bearing on the question of the

relation between syntactic representation and semantic representation. In particular, the fact that a single unambiguous surface structure can derive from more than one deep
structure source provides support for a theory which posits
a level of syntactic deep structure distinct from semantic
representation. There is no non-ad-hoc way to prevent such
a situation, and in fact there is some positive evidence for
positing a dual source for pseudo-cleft sentences, as we have
seen.

The deep structure source for clefted sentences in the
extraction theory posits an empty [Δ] in predicate position,
which is motivated on purely formal grounds: positing such
structures allows one to account for a range of facts having
to do with the shape of clefted sentences (e.g. prepositional
phrases in focus position). This sort of deep structure is
not motivated on semantic grounds, i.e. on the grounds that
it accounts for the interpretation of clefted sentences. As
we have seen, it is not at all relevant in the determination
of a significant portion of the semantic interpretation of
clefted sentences (namely, focus-presupposition relations).

The base source for copula sentences generates pseudo-
cleft sentences of a certain class, and we have proposed
that there are certain pseudo-cleft sentences which can only

be generated by this source. Thus, there are two possible sources, and we have shown that this formal distinction between two sources in deep structure plays no semantic role. This situation is logically possible only in a theory which postulates a level of syntactic deep structure, distinct from semantic representation.

FOOTNOTES TO CHAPTER 3

1. We assume here that it is possible to determine the
    referentiality of given nominal phrases. However,
    the problem of interpreting referentiality is a complex
    one, and beyond the scope of this work.

2. These facts are reflected in questions, as well:

    (i)   What is he?

          A gentleman.

          *The gentleman I know.

    (ii) Who is he?

          *A gentleman.

          The gentleman I know.

    Notice, incidentally, that referential and non-referential
    NPs are also differentiated with respect to certain
    movement rules. Consider, for example:

(2) (cont'd.)

      (iii) a. Tall though John is, he can still fit in this doorway.

          b. A gentleman though John claims to be, he always says something rude anyway.

          c. *The bank robber though John is, we don't have enough evidence to convict him yet.

As (iii) indicates, preposing across <u>though</u> can take place in predicational statements, but not specificational statements (i.e. referential NPs cannot be preposed).

3. The observations we have made here are in accord with the observation by Bach [1967] that the interpretation of the copula is a function of the semantic nature of the items which are connected by the copula. That is, the copula has a specificational interpretation when the post-copular NP is referential, and has a predicational interpretation when the post-copular item is a non-referential NP or adjective. In this sense, then, the interpretation of the copula (or, more accurately, the interpretation of the <u>sentences</u> containing the copula) is completely determined by the environment in which the copula occurs.

4. Note that not all cases involving predicate adjectives can be ambiguous, since the subject NPs in question may fail to satisfy the selectional restrictions of the adjectives. Thus:

    (i)   What John tried to be was careful.

    (ii) What John tried to be was not apparent.

(i) is interpreted only as a clefted sentences, since the predicational sense would entail that the NP what John tried to be could be a possible subject of careful. However, careful can be predicated only of human subjects. Conversely, (ii) has only the predicational sense. (If it had the specificational sense we would then expect sentences such as:

    (iii) ?John tried to be not apparent.)

Thus, ambiguities of the sort represented by (16) are possible only when the selectional restrictions of the adjective are satisfied by both the matrix NP and the embedded NP.

5. The symbol [is] for predication may in fact be a cover term which represents a series of semantic relations. For example:

    (i)   He is a fool.

    (ii) He is a doctor.

(5) (cont'd.)

While (i) represents assignment of quality, (ii) represents
a statement of class membership. However, nothing crucial
will rest on separating these various senses associated
with [is], since we need only keep these senses separate
from specification.

6. Note further that in the sense represented by (30b) it is
not possible to attach an appositive relative clause to
the NP in question:

    (i)   I don't know what he threw away; I only know
             that he threw away a valuable piece of
             equipment (*which, by the way, I need to use
             right now).

7. Such conditions would represent, of course, an absurd
complication of the grammar. Somehow it would have to be
stated that only indefinite NPs could be generated in
post-copular position, and any definite NPs found there
would have to be derived transformationally. This would
then insure that structures such as (26) would generate
only predicational statements.

8. Clifton [1969] also discusses ambiguities such as the following:

(i) What I don't eat is food for the dog.

This is paraphrased either by, "I don't eat food for the dog", or, roughly as, "What is left over is given as food for the dog". Note that the two senses are resolved when the referentiality of the initial clause is made unambiguous either way:

(ii) Whatever I don't eat is food for the dog.

(iii) The thing which I don't eat is food for the dog.

This suggests, again, that the ambiguity hinges on referentiality and not on duality of syntactic source. Furthermore, there are cases in which the ambiguity in fact appears for which one cannot, in any event, posit a dual syntactic source:

(iv) My supper is food for the dog.

This can be used either to denote the situation in which the dog food is eaten for supper, or the situation in which the supper is given to the dog as its food. Since such sentences are generated in the base and do not undergo the extraction transformation one cannot appeal to duality of source to account for the ambiguity of (iv).

9. This is assumed in order to account for selectional relations which the larger NP enters into:

   (i) I ate what he cooked.

   (ii) *I ate what he said.

10. This is, of course, true only in the very broadest sense. That is, it is not the case that the logical structure of a sentence (i.e. those aspects of meaning which have bearing on the truth conditions of a sentence) is determined _exclusively_ in deep structure. Specifically, the scope of logical elements is determined by factors of surface structure. As we point out in section 6 (especially 6.1.2 and 6.2), the scope of negation is determined by location of the focus of a sentence, and further, it can be significantly altered by variations in intonation patterns. Thus, one aspect of the logical structure of sentences determined by factors of surface structures is the scope of logical elements and certain adverbials (e.g. _even_, _only_, etc.). Aside from considerations of scope (and possibly coreferentiality), it appears that aspects of surface structures do not otherwise have bearing on the truth conditions of sentences.

11. Note also the difference in the possible scope of elements

such as _even_:

      (i)   He even called up a girl who he had met in

            Chicago.

      (ii)   He called up even a girl he had met in Chicago.

      (iii) He even called a girl up who he had met in

            Chicago.

In (i), the phrase _a girl who he had met in Chicago_ can

function as the scope of _even_, and if this is chosen as

scope then (i) is synonymous with (ii). In (iii),

predictably, this is not a possible scope of _even_. This

can be seen more clearly in the following context:

      (iv) He called up his mother, he called up his

           brother, # and he even called a girl up

           who he had met in Chicago.

Thus, the final clause of (iv) is not taken as a natural

pairing with the previous clauses, since there is no

constituent _a girl who he had met in Chicago_ which can

pair with the previous object NPs. Thus, the sentences

of (55) differ in naturalness as responses, and further

specify different foci which can act as the scope of _even_.

It must be mentioned that Lakoff [1969] states without

argument that pairs such as (55) do not differ in pre-

suppositions and do not differ in the questions they

(11) (cont'd.)

answer. But we see that there is evidence which bears on the issue, which indicates the opposite.

12. As Jackendoff points out, the use of such indices is already implied in the notation used to state transformations, in which numerals identify portions of the structure description in the structural change. Their use is also presupposed in any theory involving 'derivational constraints' (Lakoff [1969]).

13. We point out in Chapter 4 that there can be more than one focus per sentence, however, for the remainder of the discussion in this chapter we speak of the focus of a sentence.

14. Recall here the sentences of (55), which are related examples. The examples here are even clearer cases in which surface constituent structure determines the scope of even.

15. As Anderson points out, sentences such as (77b) and (78b) are not interpreted in just the same way, since in (77b) the focus is ambiguous. It could be just WATUSI, or it

(15) (cont'd.)

could be a constituent such as <u>the idea that he is tall</u>

<u>for a WATUSI</u>. Thus, in (77b) <u>even</u> has a possible scope

which it does not have in (78b).

16. The notation for questions is modified shortly.

17. Discussion of these issues and related ones is found in

Strawson [1956].

18. The expression which represents the focus is not necessar-

ily always an expression which contains a specification

relation, since it appears that foci may be represented

as predicational relations also. Consider, for example,

sentences we have discussed earlier:

(i) a. What he drew was a piece of TRASH.

b. He drew a piece of TRASH.

Recall that these sentences are both ambiguous between a

predicational and specificational sense. Taking as focus

the phrase <u>a piece of TRASH</u>, these sentences receive either

of the following representations:

(ii) a. [[he drew $\underline{x}$], [$\underline{x}$ = a piece of trash]]

b. [[he drew $\underline{x}$], [$\underline{x}$ is a piece of trash]]

Thus, if the focus constituent is a referential NP, the

(18) (cont'd.)

focus is represented as a specificational statement; if
the focus constituent is a non-referential NP, it is
represented as a predicational statement. Such representations accurately reflect, for example, that in (ib) we
do not know what was drawn, only that it was badly done,
while in (ia) we know what was drawn. Consider now the
case with adjectives:

(iii) a. What he wants his next wife to be is

FASCINATING.

b. [[he wants his next wife to be x],

[x = fascinating]].

c. [[he wants his next wife to be x],

[x is fascinating]].

Recall that sentences such as (iiia) can derive from
structures such as (20) or (21). Structures such as (20)
are interpreted as predicational statements (i.e. the
adjective fascinating is predicated of the complex subject
NP what he wants his next wife to be) and when this is
the case, the representation (iiic) is assigned to such
sentences. On the other hand, (21) does not receive a
predicational interpretation; the adjective is extracted
and moved into predicate position, but it is not interpreted as modifying the complex embedded subject. When

(18) (cont'd.)

this is the case, we assign representation (iiib) to such
sentences. This seems to be a reasonable means of accounting for such ambiguities, and indicates that foci may be
represented as relations other than specification. As far
as I can see, specification and predication are the only
semantic relations in the representation of focus.

19. The use of the expression do x as a variable here is
purely for reasons of readability. We assume that there
are semantic variables which represent given classes of
predicates and nominals, and that these can be distinguished. Since the context will make clear what sort of
variable is involved, we simply use [x] as a generalized
semantic variable. A more accurate representation for
(99b) would be: [Nixon x with Mitchell on the Cambodian
question], where x would be a predicate variable.
Furthermore, again for reasons of readability, we
represent presuppositions in essentially their surface
structure forms, but it must be kept in mind that the
presupposition is a section of a semantic reading, and
thus takes the form of a semantic reading, not a surface
structure. In short, the leftmost expression in
representations such as (99b) is intended to represent

(19) (cont'd.)

a portion of a semantic reading in which a variable occurs for some term. The forms in which such expressions are given are merely technical enough to make the point, but are not intended as precise replicas of semantic representations.

20. It should be emphasized again that the presupposition need not resemble a possible surface structure. Thus, in this case, there is no sentence which expresses the statement in the leftmost expression of (112d). At best one can paraphrase the presuppositional statement as, roughly, "The Air Force bears some relation to the action of spraying Cambodian villages". This relation is specified in the focal expression as the relation want. As Chomsky [1969] has pointed out, there is no reason to expect that semantic representations can be expressed in grammatical sentences.

21. The implication of non-uniqueness of even actually has to do with so-called natural pairing. A sentence such as:

(i)　She will even win the contest.

sets up implied contrasts with anything which could be said to pair naturally with the phrase win the contest:

(21) (cont'd.)

    (ii)   She will enter the contest, she will try her

          best, and she will even win the contest.

Sentences such as (i), however, do not imply contrasts

such as:

    (iii) She will drink some water, she will stand on

          her head, and she will even win the contest.

unless drinking water and standing on one's head are in

fact associated with the contest in some way. Thus, the

implications associated with even are not uniquely deter-

minable, since they can simply be any so-called 'natural

pairing'.

22. Note that the specific shape which the rising-falling-

rising pattern takes depends on the location of the

intonation center. Thus, consider the pseudo-cleft:

    (i)   The one who urged Nixon to appoint Carswell

          wasn't MITCHELL.

The rising-falling-rising curve here is located at the

very end of the sentence, where the intonation center is

located. Hence, the rising tone begins on the syllable

with main stress, and the falling-rising pattern which

follows is determined by how much of the sentence is left.

Thus, in (124), the rising-falling-rising pattern begins

(22) (cont'd.)

right at the beginning of the sentence, where the intonation center is located; in (125) it does not begin until
the focus constituent has been reached; and in (i) above
it does not even occur until the end of the sentence.

CHAPTER 4

FOCUS AND THE INTERPRETATION OF ANAPHORIC EXPRESSIONS

1. Focus and Anaphora

The purpose of this chapter is to discuss certain ways
in which the notation we have developed for focus-presupposition relations can be put to use in areas of the grammar
other than those we have discussed. We will attempt to show
that the notation developed in Chapter 3 plays a crucial role
in the interpretation of certain anaphoric expressions. These
anaphoric expressions include anaphoric items such as it, this,
that, thing, and so on, which appear in anaphoric expressions
such as it happens, do it, do this, do that, do the same
(thing), etc. The basic claim is that for a certain class
of expressions, the focus-presupposition relations play a crucial role in determining the readings of the pro-forms in question.

While focus-presupposition relations have a significant
effect on coreferentiality relationships involving personal
pronouns (he, she, it, etc.), it is beyond the scope of this

study to consider this area.[1] The investigation here is
limited to those pro-forms which refer to actions or propositions, rather than so-called personal pronouns. Our principal
task is the formulation of principles for interpretation of
pro-forms such as those in the following environments:

> (1) a. The US invaded Cambodia once, but <u>it</u> couldn't
>   happen again.
>
> b. The US may have destroyed Vietnam, but could the
>   US get away with <u>doing it</u> to Laos?

The position we adopt here with regard to such anaphoric
expressions is that such expressions are generated in the
base. In other words, the second clauses in (1) are generated
in essentially their surface form. We must assume that the
item <u>it</u> (and similar forms) is marked as a pro-form, and that
it has a minimal semantic feature composition to differentiate
it from other pro-forms. Such anaphoric expressions contain
no further semantic content, and thus, if the second clauses
of (1) (<u>It couldn't happen again, Could the US get away with
doing it to Laos?</u>) happen to be generated as independent sentences, their semantic representations must indicate that
there is a "gap" in such sentences. That is, in both cases
<u>it</u> refers to some action, but no specific action is referred
to.

In contexts such as those represented in (1), the pro-form

<u>it</u> (and analogous ones such as <u>this</u>, <u>that</u>, etc.) is understood as referring to some portion of the antecedent sentence. We will attempt to formulate interpretive principles by which such pro-forms are assigned semantic readings.

Consider as a background examples such as the following:

(2) a. John LECTURED Mary and then he SCOLDED the little girl.

b. JOHN lectured MARY and then HE scolded the LITTLE GIRL.

In (2a), the subject and object of the second clause are understood to be anaphoric (<u>John=he</u> and <u>Mary=the little girl</u>), however, in (2b) the subject and object of the second clause are understood to be distinct from the subject and object of the first clause. Conversely, while the two verbs in (2a) are understood to have distinct senses, in (2b) we understand them to have equivalent senses. That is, the speaker who utters (2b) is, in effect, using the verbs <u>lecture</u> and <u>scold</u> as if they were semantically equivalent. In such examples, the pairing of foci is understood as a pairing of semantically mutually exclusive items, while the pairing of non-focal material (low-stressed material) is understood as a pairing of semantically equivalent material.

By 'semantic equivalence' we do not mean synonymy, but rather a more general notion. Consider examples of the sort discussed by Lakoff [1970]:

(3) JOHN called MARY a Republican and then SHE insulted HIM.

This sentence, which has 'reciprocal contrastive stress', has an interpretation which allows the inference that to call someone a Republican is to insult him. Chomsky [1970] has suggested that the interpretive principle associated with such cases takes inputs of the following sort:

$$(4) \quad A \times B \begin{Bmatrix} \text{and} \\ \text{but} \end{Bmatrix} C \ y \ D$$

(where capital letters indicate foci, and lower case letters indicate relatively unstressed items) and associates the following interpretation with them:

(5) to $\underline{x}$ is to $\underline{y}$

This would give us for (3) the interpretation that to call someone a Republican is to insult him. Essentially, the unstressed material in such sentences is taken to be equivalent (in the sense of (5)), while the stressed material is taken to be non-equivalent.

The claim of this chapter is that the interpretation of certain anaphoric elements is a part of the general phenomenon illustrated by sentences such as those we have just discussed. Thus, consider:

(6) The Rússians torture Itálian spies and the Américans
<u>do it</u> to Albánian spies.

The paired foci, again, are interpreted as distinct, however,
the unstressed material, as before, is interpreted as equivalent in some sense. Here, the verbal expressions 'torture'
and 'do it' are relatively unstressed; further, these are
understood as equivalent in the sense that the pro-form has
the same semantic reading as the antecedent verbal expressions.
In this context, <u>do it</u> can be said to 'mean' <u>torture</u>. In
sum, when the verb of the second clause is <u>not</u> a pro-form (as
in (3)), an interpretive principle such as (5) is required.
When this verbal expression <u>is</u> a pro-form, as in (6), a
stronger sense of equivalence is required, namely that the
pro-form has the same reading as some portion of the antecedent sentence.

2. An Interpretive Principle: Pairing of Foci

Let us begin with a simple example such as:

(7) Bíll diligently studied for the exam, and Sám did it
too.

The interpretation of the second clause here is that Sam also

diligently studied for the exam. The interesting property of
such sentences is that the pro-form it (or do it) does not
refer back to the entire antecedent sentence, but refers only
to a portion of the antecedent. The portion of the reading of
the first clause which carries over to the second clause is
just that portion which includes [...studied for the exam],
and the interpretation of the pro-form of the second clause
specifically excludes the item Bill. The task before us is
to determine what principles govern such exclusion of antecedent material: how do we know which portions of the antecedent will carry over into the reading of subsequent pro-forms,
and which portions will be excluded?

I propose that the answer is given to us by the representation for focus and presupposition we have already developed on independent grounds. Thus, consider the representation of the focus-presupposition relations for the first
clause of (7), given Bill as the focus item:

(8) [[x diligently studied for the exam], [x = Bill]]
Notice that it is the representation of the presupposition
which forms precisely that portion of the reading of the first
clause which carries over into the reading of the second
clause. The claim here is that the second clause of (7)
shares this presupposition of the first clause, in that the
variable(s) of this presupposition are specified by the focus

<u>item(s) of the second clause</u>. The focus item <u>Sám</u> in the
second clause of (7) can specify the same variable of the
same presupposition which is specified by the item <u>Bíll</u> in
the first clause. In other words, sentences with the pro-
form <u>do it</u> function to provide new <u>foci</u> which specify variables
of presuppositions already present in previous clauses.

As a first approximation, then, we can represent the
meaning of the entire sentence (7) as follows:

(9) [[$\underline{x}$ diligently studied for the exam], [$\underline{x}$ = Bill]

and [$\underline{x}$ = Sam]

The expression [$\underline{x}$ = Sam] represents the semantic contribution
of the second clause of sentence (7). (We discuss in a moment
the non-focal items in such clauses, and where they fit into
representations.)

The essence of the interpretive principle we propose is
this: the principle <u>pairs foci</u> of two clauses with respect to
one given presupposition, namely the presupposition of the
more fully specified clause. When we say that the second
clause of some sentence shares the presupposition of the
first clause, we mean that the foci in the second sentence
specify the variables of this presupposition of the first
sentence. In this way, we can explain precisely which items
of the first sentence do not carry over into the interpretation of the pro-form of the second sentence: namely, all foci

of the first sentence. We will consider now more complicated
examples.

2.1. Sentences With More Than One Focus. We have implied
above that a sentence can have more than one focus constituent.
This is, in fact, possible, and shows up most clearly in contrastive sentences such as (6), where there are four distinct-
ly perceived intonation peaks. Also, quite in line with what
we have said earlier, these four constituents are interpreted
as representing novel information. Thus, the first clause of
(6) would have a representation such as:

(11) [[$\underline{x}$ torture $\underline{y}$], [$\underline{x}$ = Russians] and [$\underline{y}$ = Italians]]
Both focus constituents of the first clause are replaced by
variables, resulting in a representation such as (11).

In order to derive the reading of the second clause of
(6), the variables in the presupposition of the first clause
are now specified as those focal items which are present in
the surface form of the second clause. The following specifications are set up:

(12) [[$\underline{x}$ = Americans] and [$\underline{y}$ = Albanian spies]]
Thus, the representation for the entire sentence would look
like:

(13) [[$\underline{x}$ torture $\underline{y}$], [[$\underline{x}$ = Russians] and [$\underline{y}$ = Italian
        spies]] and [[$\underline{x}$ = Americans] and [$\underline{y}$ = Albanian spies]]]

Each set of foci is represented as a conjunction, and these two conjunctions are in turn conjoined (since the sentence itself contains the conjunction and). In representations such as (13), we interpret the symbol [,] as binding the presupposition to both sets of foci.

2.2. Shifting Intonation Centers. If what we have said so far is true, then it should be the case that shifting the intonation center in the first clause changes the readings both in the first clause and second clause. This is in fact the case. Consider examples such as the following:

(14) a. The RUSSIANS beat the Czechs but it wouldn't have happened with the POLES.

b. The Russians beat the CZECHS but it wouldn't have happened with the POLES.

In (14a) the interpretation of the second clause is that the Poles would not have beaten the Czechs. In (14b), however, the interpretation is that the Russians would not have beaten the Poles. This follows from the fact that the pairing of foci in (14) differs: in (14a) the pairing is Russians-Poles, and in (14b) the pairing is Czechs-Poles. The focus-presupposition relations in the first clauses in each case differ, as the following representation shows:

(15) a. [[x beat the Czechs], [x = the Russians]]

(15) b. [[The Russians beat $\underline{x}$], [$\underline{x}$ = the Czechs]]

Given that the second clause in sentences such as (14) shares the presupposition of the first clause, the focal item POLES in the second clause specifies either the variable in (15a) or the variable in (15b), depending on the intonation of the first clause. Hence, the ambiguity of interpretation of the second clause.

Similarly, consider cases in which the intonation center is invariant (and comes on the final constituent of the sentence), but where optional syntactic transformations have applied to alter surface constituent structure:

(16) a. The Russians beat the CZECHS, but it wouldn't have happened with the POLES.

b. The Czechs were beaten by the RUSSIANS, but it wouldn't have happened with the POLES.

The second clause in (16a) has the interpretation that the Russians wouldn't have beaten the Poles. However, in (16b) the interpretation is that the Poles wouldn't have beaten the Czechs. The representations assigned to the first clauses of (16) would be as follows:

(17) a. [[The Russians beat $\underline{x}$], [$\underline{x}$ = the Czechs]]

b. [[$\underline{x}$ beat the Czechs], [$\underline{x}$ = the Russians]]

Once again, the focal item of the second clause in each case specifies either the variable in (17a) or in (17b), depending on which presupposition is determined by the intonation pattern of the first clause.

2.3. Combining Presuppositions. Consider for a moment just the second clause in sentences such as (16):

(18) ...it wouldn't have happened to the POLES.

We have already discussed the focus constituent of this clause, POLES, noting that it specifies the variable of the presupposition of the first clause. Thus, part of the reading of this clause is the expression:

(19) [$\underline{x}$ = POLES]

Leaving aside the focus, what about the rest of the material in a clause such as (18)? Clearly the nonfocal material in (18) has a semantic interpretation, and makes a semantic contribution to the sentence as a whole (i.e. to the total reading of both clauses). In fact, the clause in (18) is an independent sentence itself, and has its own focus-presupposition relations, which can be represented as follows:

(20) [[it wouldn't have happened to $\underline{y}$], [$\underline{y}$ = POLES]]

The property of this particular reading is that it contains the pro-form it, an element which is semantically empty (though it does have a minimal set of semantic features to distinguish it from other pro-forms).

The claim here is that this pro-form is assigned a

semantic reading, namely, the presupposition of the first clause. Thus, taking (16a), the presupposition of the first clause, as shown in (17a), is as follows:

(21) [the Russians beat x]

This portion of the reading of the first clause is then assigned as the reading of the pro-form in the second clause. This operation is in essence a replacement of the pro-form by the presupposition of the previous clause. The representation of (20), with the pro-form it assigned a semantic interpretation, would then look look like:

(22) [[[the Russians beat x] wouldn't have happened

to y], [y = POLES]]

The focal item POLES not only specifies the variable of the presupposition of the second clause, but also specifies the variable of the presupposition of the first clause, which has been carried over to the second clause. Thus, an additional expression must be added to (22) to indicate this:

(23) [[[the Russians beat x] wouldn't have happened

to y], [[x = POLES] and [y = POLES]]]

Thus, the focus is a conjunction of specifications, and indicates that POLES functions as a specification within its own clause, as well as with respect to the presupposition of the first clause.

To sum up what we have said so far, we begin by considering

sentences such as (7). It is argued that in such sentences, the presence of the anaphoric element _it_ (or _do it_) in the second clause is interpreted as an indicator that the focal items of the second clause are to be interpreted as specifications of the variables of the presupposition of the first clause. Where there is more than one focal item in each clause, then there is more than one variable which is specified. The interpretation of clauses containing pro-forms involves a blending of the presupposition of the first clause with the presupposition of the second clause (i.e. the proform item in the presupposition of the second clause is replaced by the presupposition of the first clause).

This last point should be made a bit more precise. It is only those portions of the presupposition of the first clause which are _distinct_ from the presupposition of the second clause which replace the pro-form item. Consider, for example, a sentence such as:

(24) Bill believes that the world is flat, but Sám
     doesn't believe it.

The focus-presupposition relations of the second clause, with _Sam_ taken as the focus, are represented as follows:

(25) [[x believes it], [NEG [x = Sam]]]

where the scope of negation goes with the focus. In order to assign a reading to the empty pro-form element _it_, we replace

it by the presupposition of the first clause. The focus-
presupposition relations of the first clause are:

(26) [[x believes [that the world is flat]], [x = Bill]]

and thus the expression [x believes that the world is flat]
should replace the pro-form it in (25). However, the presuppositions of both clauses contain the phrase x believes, and
since this phrase in both clauses is identical, it 'cancels
out' when the presupposition of the first clause is carried
out to the second clause. Only the portion [that the world
is flat] replaces the pro-form in (25), and this is the
reading assigned to the pro-form item. When this expression
replaces the pro-form item of (25), we derive the following
representation for the second clause of (24):

(27) [[x believes [that the world is flat]], [NEG [x =
      Sam]]

Thus, if the presupposition of the first sentence happens to
contain material which is identical with material of the presupposition of the second sentence, it is canceled out when
it replaces the pro-form of the presupposition of the second
sentence.

2.4. Filtering Deviant Cases. The interpretive principle we have been developing operates in cases where there is
a pairing of foci, that is to say, cases in which intonation

peaks mark items in two clauses such that these items are
interchangeable as given specifications for a variable in a
given presupposition. Let us now consider some of the conditions under which two clauses can fail to "share" presuppositions.

Consider, first of all, sentences such as:

(28) *Jóhn read a book, but it wasn't done to Bíll.

The intonation peaks mark off the NPs John and Bill in the
two clauses, however, these are not paired foci. The reason
for this is that since they do not fulfill the same grammatical function, they cannot be interchangeable as specifications
of the same variable in a given presupposition. To see this,
consider the focus-presupposition relations of the two clauses
of (28):

(29) a. [[$\underline{y}$ read a book], [$\underline{y}$ = John]]

    b. [[it wasn't done to $\underline{x}$], [$\underline{x}$ = Bill]]

The item John specifies a variable which represents an item
which has the function of semantic agent, while the item Bill
specifies a variable which has a non-agentive function.

Recall that the notation we have been using is insuf-
ficiently precise in the sense that in an explicit representation variables representing distinct semantic functions
should themselves be formally distinct. (We have simply used
a single variable, $\underline{x}$, for convenience alone.) Thus, the focus

expressions in (29) should be explicit enough to indicate that they differ as to what sort of variable is being specified. Given such an explicit representation, one can tell by inspection that the foci of (28) do not pair, since the representations of (29) indicate that they fulfill distinct semantic functions, and thus they are not interchangeable. This predicts correctly that the sentences of (28) do not share presuppositions, and the pro-form of the second clause remains uninterpreted.

Another condition under which two clauses can fail to share a presupposition has to do with the more general property of the filtering function of semantic rules, rather than with any property of pairing. Consider, for example, a sentence such as:

(30) Jóhn ate heartily and Máry did it to Bill.

The intonation peaks mark off the NPs <u>John</u> and <u>Mary</u>, both function as semantic agents, and let us assume for the sake of argument that they are identical in semantic function. The focus-presupposition relations of both clauses would be represented as:

(31) a. [[<u>x</u> ate heartily], [<u>x</u> = John]]

b. [[<u>x</u> did it to Bill], [<u>x</u> = Mary]]

If the two foci fulfill the same grammatical function, then <u>Mary</u> is a possible specification for the variable of the

presupposition of the first clause. However, notice that
when the presupposition of the first clause is associated
with the pro-form of the second clause, we derive the following expression:

(32) [[x did [x ate heartily] to Bill], [x = Mary]]

The presupposition expression is semantically anomalous, in
the sense that sentences such as:

(33) What Mary did to Bill was eat heartily.

are anomalous. Sentences such as (30) are therefore marked
as semantically anomalous.

2.5. Cases With No Pairing of Foci. If we examine the
interpretation of anaphoric it, we see that there is a distinct difference in interpretation between those cases in
which there is pairing and those cases in which there is no
pairing. When foci are paired, then only the presupposition
of the previous clause is assigned as the reading of it; however, when there is no pairing of foci, it refers to the
entire reading of the previous sentence (i.e. includes in its
interpretation both the presupposition and foci of the previous sentence).

Consider an example such as:

(34) Naked Came the Stranger was even taken seriously by
     the critics, but one can hardly believe it.

The interpretation of the second clause here is that one can hardly believe that NCS was even taken seriously by the critics. In other words, the interpretation of it in fact includes the focus expression (i.e. derived scope of even) in its interpretation.

In the previous cases we have discussed, the foci of previous clauses are precisely those elements which are excluded. However, the difference, as we see, is that in (34) there is no pairing of foci (in our technical sense). Thus, given the focus taken seriously by the critics in the first clause, there is no presupposition of this clause such that the variables can be specified by focal items in the second clause. If the derived verb phrase is focus, the presupposition would be:

(35) [Naked Came the Stranger was x]

If the item believe in the second clause is the focus of that clause, it cannot specify the variable of the presupposition (35), since it is a predicate which cannot fill the position represented by the variable. Further, there is no other pairing, in the sense we have discussed.

We shall say, then, that when there is no pairing of foci, the anaphoric items such as it include in their readings not only presuppositions from previous clauses, but in fact the total semantic reading of previous clauses. Thus, the

representation of _it_ in (34) is the entire semantic reading
of the first clause.

Notice, incidentally, that sentences such as (34) provide
evidence that pro-forms such as _it_ include in their interpretation not only the deep structure reading of previous clauses,
but aspects of the reading of previous clauses determined by
the surface structures of such clauses (i.e. scope of 'even').

To take another case analogous to (34), consider the sentence:

(36) Bill believes that the world is flát, but Sam
doesn't belíeve it.

This sentence is identical to (24) except that here the intonation peaks fall at the end of each clause. The difference
in interpretation between (36) and (24) is significant, however. In (36) the second clause means that Sam doesn't believe that Bill believes that the world is flat. Here, again,
there is no pairing of foci; hence, no foci of the previous
clause are excluded.[2] The total reading of the previous
clause is assigned as the reading of the pro-form _it_.

3. Ross's Objections

In a recent paper, J.R. Ross [1969] has argued against a theory of the general sort proposed above, and instead maintains that the data under consideration is to be handled transformationally, by a rule known as $\underline{S}$-Deletion. We will consider his arguments here, and we hope to show that Ross's objections can be met, and further, that his proposed solutions are inadequate as they stand.

3.1. 'Sluicing'. Ross's chain of argumentation is briefly as follows. He considers the relation between sentences such as the following:

(37) a. They are going to invite someone, but I don't
   know <u>who they are going to invite</u>.

   b. They are going to invite someone, but I don't
   know <u>who</u>.

Ross refers to sentences such as (37b) as <u>sluiced</u> sentences; that is, sentences which have undergone a rule which he terms 'Sluicing', the effect of which is to delete all material from an embedded question except the preposed WH word, under identity with material in an antecedent embedded question. Hence, (37a) is mapped onto (37b).

Ross argues that sluicing must be carried out by a

syntactic deletion rule, and he argues against what he terms
an 'interpretive' theory for such sentences. On Ross' analysis, an 'interpretive theory' would posit as the underlying
form of the second clause of (37b) the following:

(38)

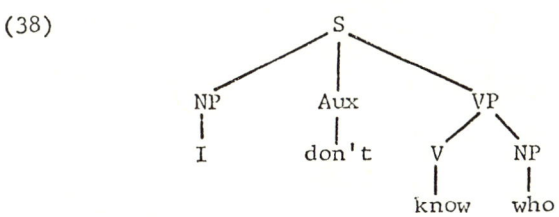

In other words, the interpretive theory which Ross sets up is
one which simply posits the surface form of such sentences as
the underlying form, and would have to provide an interpretation for such sentences in some manner.

Ross then provides a series of arguments against such an
interpretive theory, largely on the grounds that serious syntactic problems would arise. The arguments center around the
fact that an interpretive theory which posits (38) does not
recognize the WH-word who as a remnant of an embedded clause,
and Ross shows that the syntax of sentences such as (37b) requires that there be a full clause at the pre-surface level.
We will consider briefly the main arguments which Ross presents.

3.1.1. Syntactic Arguments in Favor of Sluicing. The

first argument presented has to do with the difficulty of accounting for case marking if sluiced clauses are generated in
surface form:

(39) a. They will invite someone, but I don't know whom.

b. They said someone will come, but I don't know who.

Given that the sluiced clause would be represented by (38) in
the proposed interpretive theory, it would be quite complicated to state the conditions under which the WH-word could
be marked as accusative. However, in Ross's theory, the statement of case marking is quite general, since sentences such
as (39) derive from fuller forms:

(40) a. They will invite someone, but I don't know

[Q--they will invite who]

b. They said someone will come, but I don't know

[Q--who will come]

Since the WH-word originates as an object in (40a) but a subject in (40b), it is marked as accusative in (40a), and hence
the surface form in (39a).

Ross considers next sentences such as the following:

(41) He will give us some problems on the test, but which
problems isn't clear.

If the sluiced clause is generated in surface form, there is
no non-ad-hoc way to account for the fact that the superficial
subject, which problems, which is marked as plural, does not

cause plural verb agreement; rather, there is singular verb agreement. This is not a problem in Ross's theory since the WH-word is a remnant of a full clause, and embedded clauses always cause singular verb agreement:

(42) He will give us some problems on the test, but

[Q--he will give us which problems] isn't clear.

The general form of the first two arguments is adopted for the remainder of the examples Ross presents, and we list here the more important ones:

(43) She's eating some apples, but I wonder how many apples.

(44) a. We know that he was eating, but what isn't clear.

b. We know that he was eating but it isn't clear what.

Consider the problems involved if it is claimed that the sluiced clauses in each case are generated in surface form. If, in (43), the sluiced clause I wonder how many apples is generated as such, with the phrase how many apples as an object NP, then how can one account for the fact that sentences such as the following are impossible:

(47) *I wonder apples.

which also has an object NP after the verb wonder. Clearly, wonder does not take object NPs of this sort, and in a theory such as Ross's this fact is explained by deriving (43) from:

(48) She's eating some apples, but I wonder [Q--she is

eating how many apples]

Finally, the examples of (44) indicate that the sluiced
clauses can undergo extraposition. On Ross's theory this
would be accounted for, since a full embedded clause appears:

(49) a. We know that he was eating, but [it $_S$[Q--he was

eating what]$_S$] isn't clear.

b. We know that he was eating, but it isn't clear

$_S$[Q--he was eating what]$_S$

If sluiced clauses such as those of (44) are generated in
surface form, however, stating the extraposition process
would be quite complicated since, presumably, one would need
to allow for the possibility of NP extraposition as well as
S extraposition.[3]

On the basis of facts such as the ones we have discussed,
Ross concludes that sluiced clauses must be derived by a deletion transformation. Having established this point, Ross then
presents a transformational theory for anaphoric expressions.

3.2. The Transformational Approach: Syntactic Deletion.
Ross begins by considering sentences of the following sort:

(50) Harold scratched his arm and so did I.
This sentence, as Ross notes, can have either of the following interpretations:

(51) a. Harold$_i$ scratched his$_i$ arm and I$_j$ scratched his$_i$
      arm too.

   b. Harold$_i$ scratched his$_i$ arm and I$_j$ scratched my$_j$
      arm too.

If sentence (50) is to be derived by a deletion rule which
deletes an occurrence of a verb phrase in the second clause
under identity with a verb phrase in the first clause, then,
as Ross argues, there is a problem in deriving (51b), since
the first phrase is <u>scratch his$_i$ arm</u> while the second verb
phrase is <u>scratch my$_j$ arm</u>.

   In order to delete the second verb phrase of (50b) 'under
identity with' the verb phrase in the first clause, some condition must be placed on the definition of identity which
allows the difference in pronouns in this case to be overlooked. Ross proposes a notion of 'sloppy identity' which is
essentially that given in Ross [1967, §5.2.3.1]:

(52) "Constituents are identical if they have the same
      constituent structure and are identical morpheme-
      for-morpheme, or if they differ only as to pronouns,
      where the pronouns in each of the identical consti-
      tuents are commanded by antecedents in the non-
      identical portions of the phrase marker."

Thus, sloppy identity means, essentially, that commanded pronouns are overlooked in determining identity relationships.

Ross then argues that since it is necessary to have a notion of sloppy identity, it is then possible to derive sentences with anaphoric _it_ by a rule of _S-Deletion_, along with properly constructed deep structures. For example, in Ross's framework, a sentence such as (6) would derive from a structure such as that shown in (53). The surface form of (6) can be derived by deleting S^5 under sloppy identity with S^4: even though the pronouns in the two embedded sentences differ, they are overlooked in determining identity because they are commanded by antecedents.

(53)

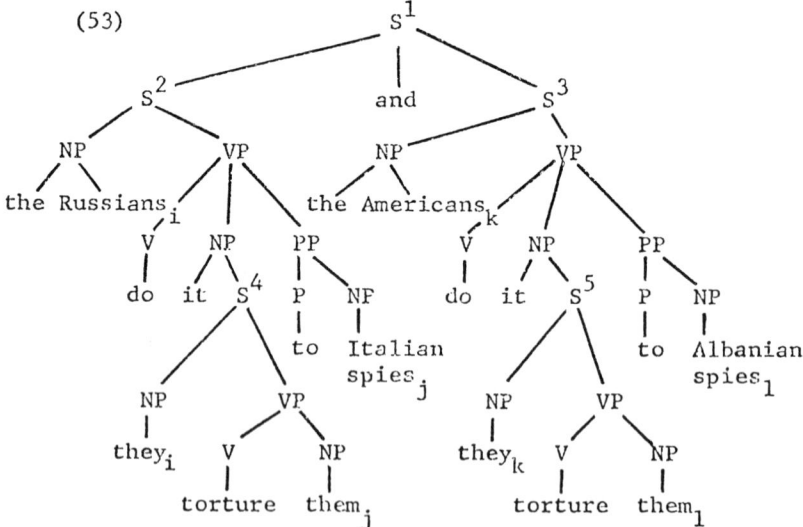

As Ross points out, such evidence is insufficient to demonstrate that the general class of sentences illustrated by (6) _must_ be derived by deletion rules which operate on a

condition of sloppy identity. Showing that (6) <u>can</u> derive
from structures such as (53) by a deletion rule does not show
that such sentences <u>cannot</u> be accounted for by interpretive
principles. If it can be shown that deletion under sloppy
identity <u>must</u> be involved in at least some cases (i.e. if <u>any</u>
theory must posit deletion under sloppy identity for some
case), then, since deletion under sloppy identity can generalize to handle other cases, it will be shown that interpretive rules are superfluous and are not required.

Ross claims to have such a case in the following sentence:

> (54) (=Ross's (55)) Bob knows how to crane his neck, but
> I don't know how.

Ross argues that since this sentence has a sluiced clause,
and since it has been shown that sluiced clauses must be derived by deletion, therefore, the sluiced clause of (54) derives by deletion. Given the meaning of the second clause,
sloppy identity must be involved (in that the deleted VP is
<u>crane my neck</u>, which must delete under identity with <u>crane</u>
<u>his neck</u>).

Ross acknowledges that one could answer this argument
by claiming that the underlying VP in question is actually
<u>crane neck</u>, until some post-deletion stage at which the pos-
sessive pronoun would be filled in. This would render

superfluous the notion of sloppy identity. He then argues
that this is not possible, due to sentences such as the
following:

> (55) (=Ross's (64)) I know how to say I'm sorry, and
> Bill knows how, too.

The second clause has the interpretation, "Bill knows how to
say he's sorry." This means that the deleted VP to say he's
sorry must have deleted under sloppy identity with the VP in
the first clause. Ross argues that one cannot claim that the
personal pronoun does not appear in these expressions, since,
[p. 274], "...it is obviously unlikely that the subject of
be sorry does not appear in deep structure, being filled in
only later." Thus, deletion under sloppy identity is required, and, since such deletion can handle other cases involving anaphoric expressions (given properly constructed
deep structure forms), interpretive principles are not
needed.[4,5]

3.3. "Sloppy Identity". The crucial step in Ross's
argument is to establish the necessity of so-called 'sloppy
identity'. If there is no notion of sloppy identity, then
the rule of S-Deletion cannot be extended to cover sentences
such as (6), (since in structures such as (53), the sentence
to be deleted is not identical with the sentence which is its

antecedent). Clearly, then, it is not merely the existence
of syntactic deletion rules which poses a threat to an interpretive theory, rather, the existence of deletion rules along
with a notion of sloppy identity renders interpretive principles unnecessary. However, the notion of sloppy identity
as Ross states is inadequate, in that it makes false predictions about the range of possible ambiguities.

    3.3.1. Defects in the Notion of Sloppy Identity. First
of all, we can note that sloppy identity is not necessary
for most of the cases which Ross discusses. Phrases such as
crane one's neck or scratch one's arm (which involve a distinction of alienable/inalienable possession) can be derived
from underlying structures of the form crane the neck and
scratch the arm. Hence, a sentence such as (50) could derive
from either of the following:

    (56) a. Harold scratched the arm and I scratched the arm.

        b. Harold scratched his arm and I scratched his arm.
Deletion could operate in either case, and no notion of sloppy
identity would be necessary.

    There is, by the way, positive evidence for representa-
tions such as (56a). As Michael Helke has pointed out [per-
sonal communication] the definite article appears in expressions such as:

(57) He hit me on the arm.

(58) It is difficult to crane the neck.

Thus, in a sentence such as (54), it is not necessary that there be a notion of sloppy identity involved.

If we turn to (55), it seems to me that similar considerations are involved here. This sentence has only the interpretation that Bill knows how to say he is sorry, and cannot have an interpretation such that Bill knows how to say I am sorry. In other words, the expression to say one is sorry is an idiomatic reflexive expression, with a meaning equivalent to a phrase such as to excuse oneself. Hence, it may very well be that the subject of such a phrase, if it is in fact reflexive, would not be specified at the deep structure level. I have no wish to press this point, however, since it is possible to find cases where there are no idiomatic possessive expressions, and where there are ambiguities of the sort Ross intends:

(59) John knows why he is sick but Bill doesn't know why.

This can have either of the following readings:

(60) a. $John_i$ knows why he_i is sick but $Bill_j$ doesn't know why he_j is sick.

b. $John_i$ knows why he_i is sick but $Bill_j$ doesn't know why he_i is sick.

Thus, it would appear that sloppy identity is necessary for such cases. Before discussing these particular cases, however, let us consider in what ways sloppy identity fails.

Basically, the notion of sloppy identity, as Ross has stated it, is too unconstrained. The notion as it stands predicts that the sort of ambiguity we have discussed should occur in a much wider range of cases than it actually does. Consider, for example, a sentence such as:

(61) John feared that he had cancer, but I didn't mention it to Mary.

This sentence is unambiguous, the second clause having the interpretation that I did not mention to Mary that John feared that he had cancer. However, on Ross's hypothesis, there ought to be two further readings, namely, that I did not mention to Mary that I had cancer; or, that I did not mention to Mary that she had cancer. These two readings are possible since (61) can have the following sort of representation in Ross's theory:

(62)

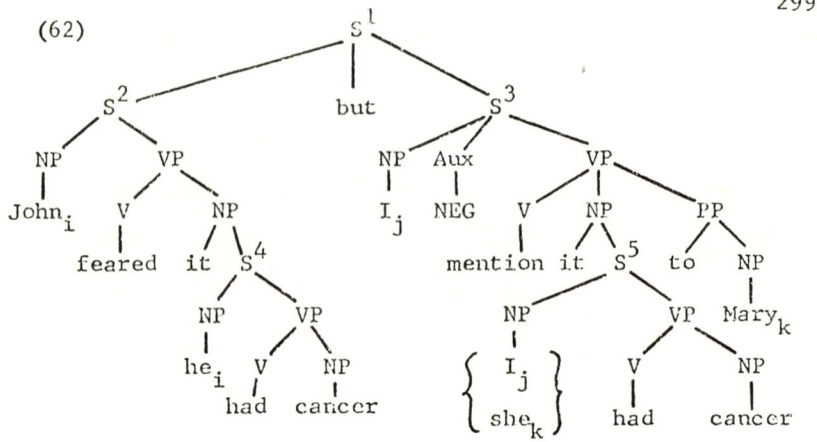

The embedded sentence S^5 can delete under sloppy identity with S^4 since the pronoun subjects (whether I_j or she_k) are commanded by antecedents in the higher sentence S^3. Hence, deletion under sloppy identity allows a greater range of ambiguities than is actually the case.

Note, of course, that as further NPs are added to sentences such as (61), the theory of sloppy identity predicts a proportionately increasing range of ambiguities. Consider, for example:

(63) John feared that he had cancer, but I told Mary not to mention it to John's mother or John's father.

Again, (63) is unambiguous, and has the interpretation that I cautioned Mary not to mention that John feared that he had cancer. Ross's theory, however, predicts that (63) is five ways ambiguous. It can have the reading just mentioned; it

can have the two further readings derivable in the manner of
(62) (i.e. where $\underline{I}$ or $\underline{Mary}$ command the pronoun subject in the
embedded sentence S^5); and finally, it can have the two addi-
tional readings derivable in case the NPs $\underline{John's\ mother}$ or
$\underline{John's\ father}$ command anaphoric pronouns in the subject position of the embedded sentence S^5.

If we consider ways in which to constrain the notion of
sloppy identity, we are led to a theory which makes use of the
notion of pairing. If we examine what properties of (61) pre-
clude the ambiguities in question, we note that in (61) there
is $\underline{no}$ pairing of foci in the sense we have discussed. That
is, there are no pairings in (61) such that the focal items
in question are $\underline{interchangeable}$ as specifications for the same
semantic variable representing a given semantic function.
For example, even if the NPs $\underline{John}$ and $\underline{I}$ were to form intonation peaks, these items would not be paired foci, since each
fulfills a distinct semantic function. The NP $\underline{I}$ in the
second clause has an agentive function, while the NP $\underline{John}$ has
a non-agentive function, hence, these two items do not specify the same semantic variables.

As discussed in section 2.5., in cases in which there is
no pairing of foci, the anaphoric expression is assigned the
total semantic reading of the previous clause (i.e. no elements are omitted). Thus, in (61) the reading assigned to

the pro-form is the reading of the entire antecedent clause, i.e. <u>John feared that he had cancer</u>. This is, in fact, the correct reading in this case.[6] The significant property in (61), then, is the <u>lack</u> of pairing.

Sloppy identity would operate, of course, in just those cases where foci happen to be paired. In order to constrain its operation, some equivalent of a pairing principle would have to-be built in. Otherwise, there would be no way to account for pairs such as those of (14) and (16), as well as the difference between (24) and (36).

4. An Interpretive Approach to Pronoun Ambiguities

To return now to cases such as (59), we ask how these are to be accounted for within the framework we propose ((59) is repeated here as (64)):

(64) John knows why he is sick but Bill doesn't know why.
The most obvious condition which we can impose is the follow-ing:

(65) If some item is chosen as focus and is replaced by
a variable in the semantic reading, then all following pronominal references to the focus item can also

Thus, in (64), if the item John is chosen as focus, and is
replaced by a variable, then the following pronominal reference he can optionally be replaced by a variable as well.
Thus, either of the presuppositions, [x said that he$_i$ was
sick] or [x said that x was sick] can be formed. The focus
of the second clause, Bill, can thus fill either the single
variable position, or both variable positions.

4.1. Intonation and Pronoun Ambiguities. I should point
out here, however, that at least for my own speech intonational phenomena are, again, relevant to the determination of
the presuppositions in question. Consider the fully specified
paraphrase form of (64); it can have either of the following
intonation patterns:

(66) a. Jóhn knows why hé is sick but Bíll doesn't know
        why hé is sick.

     b. Jóhn knows why hĕ is sick but Bíll doesn't know
        why hĕ is sick.

(66a) has the interpretation in which Bill doesn't know why
Bill is sick, while (66b) has the interpretation that Bill
doesn't know why John is sick. Where the personal pronoun he
refers to distinct persons, then it has stress in each case;
where the personal pronoun refers to the same person, it is

unstressed in both cases.

This stress pattern is brought out even more clearly in sentences such as:

(67) a. Jóhn knows why hé is sick but Máry doesn't know why shé is sick.

b. Jóhn knows why hĕ is sick but Máry doesn't know why hĕ is sick.

Even though there could be no chance of confusion as to the reference of the personal pronoun, the stress patterns on such sentences is still obligatory. When we consider the reduced forms, as with (64), we note that the same pattern is present. Consider, for example:

(68) a. Jóhn knows why hé is sick but Máry doesn't know why.

b. Jóhn knows why hĕ is sick but Máry doesn't know why.

The first sentence, (68a), has the interpretation that Mary doesn't know why Mary is sick, while the second sentence has the interpretation that Mary doesn't know why John is sick.

The focus-presupposition relations which would be assigned to such sentences would be derived by replacing stressed items with variables, while leaving unstressed items intact:

(69) a. [[$\underline{x}$ knows why $\underline{y}$ is sick], [$\underline{x}$=John$_i$] and [$\underline{y}$=he$_i$]]

b. [[$\underline{x}$ knows why he$_i$ is sick], [$\underline{x}$=John$_i$]]

Taking Mary as the focus of the second clause, it specifies either both variables in (69a), or it specifies just one variable in (69b). Hence, there is a dual reading of such sentences.

The same considerations hold for previous examples we have discussed. For example, note the intonation pattern on sentences such as:

(70) a. Jóhn scratched his arm and Í scratched my arm.

b. Jóhn scratched hĭs arm and Í scratched hĭs arm.

This same pattern carries over in sentences such as:

(71) a. Jóhn scratched his arm and Í did too.

b. Jóhn scratched hĭs arm and Í did too.

In one case, the presupposition of the first clause contains two variable positions to be specified, while in the other case the presupposition contains only one variable position to be specified.

Finally, we can take a more complicated example, such as:

(72) a. Jóhn thinks that hís father hates hím and Máry thinks that hér father hates hér.

b. Jóhn thinks that hĭs father hates hĭm and Máry thinks that hĕs father hates hĭm.

Compare the sentences of (72) with those of (73):

(73) a. Jóhn thinks that hís father hates hím and Máry does too.

(73) b. Jóhn thinks that hís father hates hím and Máry

   does too.

Once again, when intonation peaks mark off more than one focus, then the presupposition contains more than one variable position which can be filled by the focus of the second sentence.

For such cases, we need to modify condition (65) as follows (which, by the way, is required in <u>any</u> theory):

(74) Given an antecedent and a string of pronominal

   forms which are coreferential with that antecedent,

   if one of the pronominal forms is taken as a focus

   and is replaced by a variable in the reading, then

   <u>all</u> the pronominal forms must be replaced by vari-

   ables, whether these have intonation peaks or not.

This is simply to express the fact that there are no readings for sentences such as (73a) in which the second clause could mean something like, "Mary thinks that Mary's father hates John." Thus, with respect to an antecedent and subsequent pronominal references to this antecedent, the theory needs an "all or none" condition with respect to the pronominal references: either all are pulled out and replaced by variables, or none are.

   4.1.1. <u>Perceptual Cues for Intonation Peaks</u>. In discus-sing intonational phenomena and the role which intonation

plays in marking foci, it must be stressed that the intonation peaks on the pronouns in sentences we have been discussing need <u>not</u> be perceived as loud contrastive stress peaks.
To establish a pronominal item as focal it is sufficient that
the item be relatively more prominent than the surrounding
material, and, in fact, stress on pronouns (as in (71a)) is
just heavy enough to differentiate them minimally from the
unstressed, pro-clitic pronominal forms (as in (71b)).

It is reasonable to assume that intonation peaks are perceived relative to the pitch levels of surrounding material,
and thus an intonation peak, in this sense, need not represent heavy stress, in some absolute sense. It seems also
that there are other cues in the speech signal which indicate
the intonational structure of a sentence. Consider in this
regard a fact pointed out by James McCawley [MIT lecture,
spring, 1970] that in unstressed third person pronouns, the
initial <u>h</u> drops, while in stressed pronouns it does not.
Thus, in (71b) the pronoun <u>his</u> is heard as [iz], while in
(71a) the pronoun is heard as [hiz]. This, then, functions
as a cue that the pronoun is unstressed in one case, while
stressed in the other, even though there may not be a perceived stress peak on the pronoun in (71a).

4.2. Cases with Two or More Anaphoric Expressions. Interesting confirmation for the interpretive approach is found
in a class of sentences in which there is more than one anaphoric expression. For example, consider the following case
[examples of this general form are due to Edward Whitten, in
personal communication to Morris Halle]:

(75) John always tells people that he is sick, and al-

though Max does it also, Mary doesn't do it.

The interpretation of the two elliptical clauses is either
(a) although Max also always tells people that John is sick,
Mary doesn't tell people that John is sick, or, (b) although
Max also always tells people that he (Max) is sick, Mary
doesn't tell people that she (Mary) is sick. In other words,
each additional anaphoric clause has the understood pronominal references coreferential with its own surface subject, or
coreferential with the subject of the initial clause in the
series of clauses which make up the whole sentence. Thus,
for example, the final clause of (75) cannot have the interpretation that Mary doesn't tell people that Max is sick.

This state of affairs is predicted by the interpretive
theory, for the following reasons. The initial clause of (75),
in a manner we have already discussed, receives either of the
following representations:

(76) a. [x always tells people that he$_i$ is sick]

(76) b. [x always tells people that x is sick]

The variables in these presuppositions are specified by the focal items in the subsequent anaphoric clauses. Thus, if presupposition (76a) is chosen, then all following focal items specify just the subject variable; hence, for the second clause we form [Max_j tells people that he_i is sick], and for the third clause we form [$Mary_k$ doesn't tell people that he_i is sick]. If presupposition (76b) is chosen, then for the second clause we form [Max_j tells people that Max_j is sick], and for the third clause we form [$Mary_k$ doesn't tell people that $Mary_k$ is sick].

In other words, in the system we have proposed, it is the case that only the _first_ clause determines the form of the presuppositions, because the other following clauses are generated with anaphoric expressions and _not_ with the fully specified set of antecedents and pronouns. Since the presuppositions of the first clause are carried over into the following clauses, it simply follows that each additional clause will either have pronominal references coreferential with its own subject, _or_ coreferential with _just the subject of the initial clause_. For example, it is impossible to derive the reading [$Mary_k$ doesn't tell people that Max_j is sick] because there is no presupposition [x tells people that Max_j is sick].

In a theory with deletion under sloppy identity, however,

it is possible to derive the impossible reading. Consider
the following representations:

(77) a. Clause 1: [John$_i$ tells people [he$_i$ is sick]]

   b. Clause 2: [Max$_j$ tells people [he$_j$ is sick]]

   c. Clause 3: [Mary$_k$ doesn't tell people [he$_j$ is
      sick]]

Deletion can occur in Clause 2 (to produce Max does it),
since the commanded pronoun can be overlooked. Deletion
occurs in Clause 3, since the pronoun is identical with the
pronoun in Clause 2. This derivation would thus allow the
impossible interpretation: "John always tells people that he
is sick, and although Max tells people that he (Max) is sick,
Mary doesn't tell people that Max is sick." Once again, a
theory with deletion under sloppy identity makes false predictions.

5. Deletion Rules and Interpretive Rules

We have seen that the notion of sloppy identity is not
sufficiently constrained, and that some equivalent of a
theory which utilizes the notion of pairing of foci must be
employed. At this point let us consider what happens if

sloppy identity is eliminated altogether.

First of all, this would mean that the rule of S-Deletion could not be used to derive sentences such as (6), or sentences of that general sort. The reason for this, as we have seen, is that the embedded sentences to be deleted often have no antecedents which are strictly identical with them. Let us then propose that S-Deletion be eliminated entirely, since, in the absence of sloppy identity, there is a significant range of cases for which it would not work. If S-Deletion is eliminated, the pro-forms in question would be handled interpretively: they would be generated in the base, and supplied a semantic interpretation by principles discussed in section 2.

Recall here that the rule of S-Deletion is used to derive sentences which have pro-form remnants, such as it. This rule is used to derive sentences which contain anaphoric expressions such as do it, mention it, it happens, and so on. By eliminating S-Deletion, this means that sentences which contain actual pro-form items such as it are handled interpretively. We must ask now what happens with cases such as (64), (71), and (73), in which there are no pro-form remnants, but which contain so-called 'elliptical' clauses.

Such clauses are derived by deletion rules, namely VP-Deletion and Sluicing. These rules have the effect of

deleting syntactic material without leaving behind any pro-
form traces (i.e. the clauses can be said to contain $\emptyset$ as a
"pro-form"). The rules of VP-Deletion and Sluicing account
for a significant range of syntactic facts (cf. Ross [1969]
for discussion of VP-Deletion), and if one were to abandon
such rules then it would have to be shown that the syntactic
facts mentioned by Ross could be handled in some natural
fashion.

5.1. Compatibility of Deletion Rules and Interpretive
Principles. It seems to me that it is not necessary to
eliminate such rules, and that, in fact, the question here is
irrelevant. Consider, in this regard, the following sort of
example:

(78) a. Jack left early and Mary did too.

b. Jack left early and Mary left early too.

Let us assume that there is a rule of VP-Deletion, which
operates on (78b) to produce (78a). If (78b) is the deep
structure source for (78a), then part of the reading for (78a)
will be the grammatical relations determined on (78b). Recall,
however, that focus-presupposition relations are determined
by factors of surface structure representations, and therefore, the interpretive principle for focus will operate on
the surface form (78a), whether or not this has been derived

by deletion.

Even if we assume that (78a) has been derived by deletion, the interpretive principle for focus operates on the
surface form (78a). With regard to the second clause, it
marks the constituent Mary as focus. Having located the
focus constituent as Mary, it operates on the reading which
has been assigned from the deep structure, and forms expressions for focus and presupposition, as we have discussed.
Thus, the existence of a rule of VP-Deletion is in no way inconsistent with the interpretive theory we have proposed,
since the focus-presupposition relations will be read off
the surface form in any event.

Naturally, the crux of the problem has to do with sentences such as:

(79) John said that he was sick, and Mary did too.

If there is no notion of sloppy identity, and if (79) derives
by VP-Deletion, then there is only one source for such a sentence:

(80) John$_i$ said that he$_i$ was sick and Mary$_j$ said that
   he$_i$ was sick.

How can we then account for the other reading of (79), namely,
where the second clause means "Mary said that she was sick"?

We will make a tentative proposal here, to the following
effect:

(81) In sentences in which deletion has occurred in the
second clause (such as (77)), if the second clause
shares a presupposition with the first clause (i.e.
if the focus of the second clause and the focus of
the first clause are interchangeable as specifications of some variable of a presupposition of the
first clause), then this particular presupposition
is assigned as part of the reading of the second
clause.

Recall that (79) is assigned the reading of (80) since it
derives from (80). The other reading of (79) is derived as
follows: there is a presupposition of the first clause, [x
said that x was sick], which is shared by the second clause
(in the sense just discussed). Therefore, we assign this
presupposition to the second clause, and with the item Mary
as focus, we would have:

(82) [[x said that x was sick], [x = Mary]]

In other words, this would be the reading, "Mary said that
Mary was sick."

To sum up briefly: if there is a rule of VP-Deletion, but
no notion of sloppy identity, then some means must be devised
to account for ambiguous readings (for which the notion of
sloppy identity was originally introduced). The proposal advanced to handle these cases is one in which the second clause

is assigned as part of its reading any presupposition which
it shares with the first clause. This is in essence to claim
that deletion is not "meaning preserving", in the sense that
the output form of deletion rules can have a semantic interpretation not associated with the input form of such rules.
We are claiming here that the output of deletion rules can be
assigned additional semantic information, which derives from
antecedent clauses, and which is not present at all in the
pre-deletion stage.

5.2. Evidence that Deletion is not Meaning Preserving.
It should be pointed out here that this approach is more than
just a means of eliminating sloppy identity. It can be shown
that this general approach must be adopted. The argument
against the sloppy identity approach becomes decisive when
we note that there is independent evidence that clauses which
have undergone deletion must be assigned semantic information
from preceding clauses. This has been pointed out by Chomsky
[class lectures, 1969] in connection with sentences such as
the following:

(83) a. John hasn't been here for 2 weeks.

b. Bill has been here for 2 weeks.

As Chomsky has noted, (83a) has the interpretation that at
no point in time during the previous 2 weeks has John been

here. However, the interpretation of the temporal expression in (83b) is that for the <u>duration</u> of two weeks Bill has been here. Let us call the interpretation of the temporal expression in (83a) 'non-durative' and that in (83b) 'durative'. The crucial fact here is that (83b) cannot have a non-durative sense.

However, notice now a sentence such as (84):

(84) John hasn't been here for two weeks, but Bill has.

The interpretation of (84) is that at no point during the previous two weeks has John been here, but that at some <u>point</u> during the last two weeks Bill <u>has</u> been here. What is striking is that the second clause <u>cannot</u> have a durative interpretation; however, if VP-Deletion has applied in the derivation of the second clause, its underlying form must be (83b).

An example such as (81) shows that with a rule of VP-Deletion, additional semantic principles must be posited in any event to account for the fact that the clause which forms the output of deletion is assigned semantic information from the antecedent clause. We conclude that an interpretive approach, which would allow the output of deletion rules to be assigned additional semantic information from the antecedent clause, gains significant support from sentences such as (84).

6. Summary

In the first section of this chapter we propose an interpretive approach to account for the interpretation of a class of anaphoric expressions. The interpretive principles involved assign various interpretations to anaphoric expressions on the basis of presence or absence of pairing of foci.

When we examine the approach proposed by Ross, we note that the notion of sloppy identity is not sufficiently constrained. We argue that any theory must utilize a notion of pairing of foci in surface structure in order to explain just which portions of antecedent sentences are excluded from the interpretation of anaphoric expressions. If sloppy identity is abandoned, we ask whether deletion rules should also be abandoned.

We argue that this is not necessary, and that ambiguities of the sort represented by (79) can be accounted for by having interpretive principles operate on the output of deletion rules. This is justified on the basis of the fact that interpretive rules for focus-presupposition relations will operate on surface structure in any event (i.e. will only operate on the output of deletion rules). Furthermore, sentences such as (84) indicate that clauses which have

presumably undergone deletion will have to be assigned semantic information from previous clauses; this example, is,
furthermore, independent of any considerations of the sort
of ambiguity which motivates sloppy identity. Our claim is
that in such a system interpretive rules would not "duplicate"
the work of deletion rules, but rather, interpretive rules
supplement deletion rules.

FOOTNOTES TO CHAPTER 4

1. It has been noted in recent work (cf. Akmajian and
    Jackendoff [1970] and Lakoff [1968]) that stress levels
    play a significant role in determining coreferentiality
    relationships, particularly in that items which enter
    into coreferentiality relationships are typically un-
    stressed, i.e. non-focal. Thus, consider cases with de-
    scriptions:

    (i) a. After Herb bought some gásoline, that dirty
           Maoist made a Molotov cócktail.

        b. After Herb bought some gasoline, that dirty
           Máoist made a Molotov cocktail.

    In (ib) where the description that dirty Maoist contains
    the intonation center, it is not taken as being coreferen-
    tial with the constituent Herb, as it is in (ia).

        Along these lines, both Postal [1968, Chapter 19]

and Lakoff [1968] have noted a distinction in sentences
such as the following, with respect to the coreferentiality
relationship involved:

(ii) a. John will sháve himself.

b. The one John will shave is himself.

They note that in (iia) it is presupposed that John and
himself are coreferential, while in (iib) it is asserted
that John and himself are coreferential. Note that this
basic distinction correlates with another factor in these
sentences, namely, that the anaphoric expression is the
focus in (iib), but is part of the presupposition in (iia).
Thus, the interpretive system we propose in Chapter 3
automatically assigns the pronoun as part of the presupposition in (iia), and assigns it as part of the assertion of specification of the variable in (iib):

(iii) a. [[John will $\underline{x}$ himself], [$\underline{x}$ = sháve]]

b. [[John will shave $\underline{x}$], [$\underline{x}$ = himself]]

Note that the same interpretation of asserted coreferentiality is present in sentence (iia) when the pronoun bears the intonation center:

(iv) John will shave HIMSELF.

In this sentence, too, it is not presupposed, but rather
asserted, that John and himself are coreferential. Since
our system assigns the representation (iiib) to (iv), (as

well as (iib)), it accounts for the fact that the interpretation of asserted coreferentiality is present when
the anaphoric expression bears the intonation center.

The conditions on asserted coreferentiality differ
from conditions on presupposed coreferentiality. This
can be seen from examples such as the following:

(v) a. The one John wants Bill to describe is
himsélf.

b. The one John wants Mary to describe is himsélf.

c. The one John wants Mary to shave is himsélf.

d. The one John claimed had been cheated was
himsélf.

e. The one I thought Mary had baked the cake
for was mysélf.

In (va) the reflexive pronoun can be coreferential with
either of the preceding NPs; that it can be coreferential
with John is brought out clearly in the next two sentences. Note, however, that none of the sentences of (v)
have paraphrases of the following sort:

(vi)a. John wants Bill to describe himself.

b. *John wants Mary to describe himself.

c. *John wants Mary to shave himself.

d. *John claimed that himself had been cheated.

(vi) e. *I thought that Mary had baked the cake for myself.

(via) is unambiguous (the reflexive refers only to <u>Bill</u>), and thus is not a paraphrase for (va). The rest of the sentences are ungrammatical. All except for (vid) can, however, be improved by addition of stress on the reflexive:

(vii) a. John wants Bill to describe HIMSELF.

   b. John wants Mary to describe HIMSELF (not BILL)

   c. John wants Mary to shave HIMSELF (not BILL)

   d. I thought that Mary had baked the cake for MYSELF (not BILL)

Furthermore, such sentences are acceptable with so-called 'emphatic reflexive forms', that is, forms such as <u>he</u> <u>himself</u>.

These examples are raised to illustrate that intonation has significant effect on coreferentiality relationships. Exactly what the conditions are on asserted coreferentiality is a question which extends beyond the scope of this thesis.

2. That is, given the intonation pattern indicated, the focus of the first clause of sentence (36) is the predicate

flat. Replacing this item with a variable gives us the presupposition expression:

(i) [Bill believes that the world is x]

The focus of the second clause of (36) is the verb believe. Notice that this focus expression cannot specify the variable of the presupposition (i), i.e. a predicate such as believe cannot fill this position. Hence, the focal expressions of (36) do not pair, in the intended sense, and this accounts for the difference in interpretation between this case and sentence (24).

3. Note that Ross's arguments against what he terms an 'interpretive' theory are predicated on the assumption that such a theory posits for sluiced clauses their minimal surface forms, as in (38). If this assumption is abandoned, many of the arguments are overcome. For example, in the sort of framework we have adopted in this study, it is possible to have "empty" nodes in phrase markers, i.e. lexical insertion is optional (recall the empty predicate node in the source for clefted sentences). In this sort of theory, phrase markers such as (ii) can be generated for sentences such as (i):

(i) Someone ate the cheese, but I don't know who.

(ii)

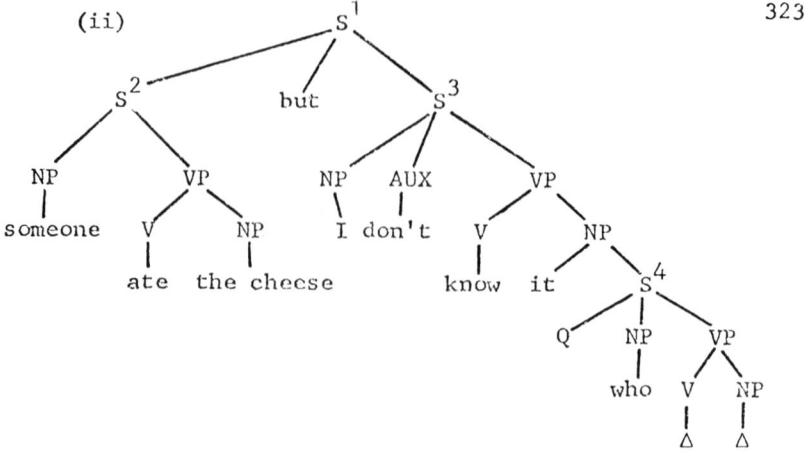

Given this sort of structure, then many of Ross's
arguments no longer hold. Case marking can be accounted
for, in that the WH word could originate either as subject
or non-subject in clauses such as S^4. The problem connected with verbal agreement patterns ((41)) is no longer
relevant, since a full embedded clause is posited in
structures such as (ii). Similarly, the problem represented by (43) is no longer relevant, since a full clause
complement would be generated as object of wonder, and not
just a single NP. Finally, extraposition could apply in
the normal fashion, since in sentences such as (44) the
second clause would have a full clause in which the interrogative pronoun would be embedded.

There are, however, arguments which Ross presents
which the theory sketched here does not overcome. First,

Ross notes the following pattern:

(iii) I know he has a picture of somebody, but I

don't know
$\left\{\begin{array}{l}\text{who} \\ \text{of whom} \\ \text{*a picture of whom}\end{array}\right\}$

This follows from the pattern associated with embedded questions:

(iv) I don't know
$\left\{\begin{array}{l}\underline{\text{who}}\text{ he has a picture of} \\ \underline{\text{of whom}}\text{ he has a picture} \\ \underline{\text{*a picture of whom}}\text{ he has}\end{array}\right\}$

Assume that an interpretive theory were to posit for the second clause of (iii) the following structure:

(v)

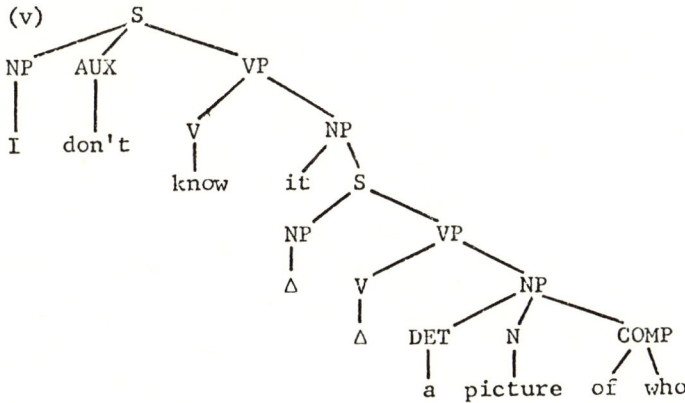

Given this structure, it would be possible to partially predict the pattern given in (iv), i.e., the full NP could not prepose, since it never does in such embedded questions.

The problem, however, is that it should be possible to prepose the WH word in the embedded clause of (v). However, this produces an ungrammatical sentence:

(vi) *I know he has a picture of somebody, but I

don't know of whom a picture.

The other argument which Ross presents which has no obvious solution in the revised interpretive theory presented here has to do with the fact that in embedded questions prepositional phrases cannot be fronted when the preposition is part of an idiomatic expression. For example:

(vii) a. Who are you going to do away with?

b. *With whom are you going to do away?

The same facts hold for sluiced clauses:

(viii) a. Bill is going to do away with someone, but

I don't know who.

b. *Bill is going to do away with someone,

but I don't know with whom.

These facts are easily stateable if the sluiced clause derives from a full embedded question, since the idiomatic expression will be present in the pre-deletion form of the sentence.

The problem for the interpretive approach, however, is that in a structure such as the following (for the second clause of the sentences of (viii)):

(ix)

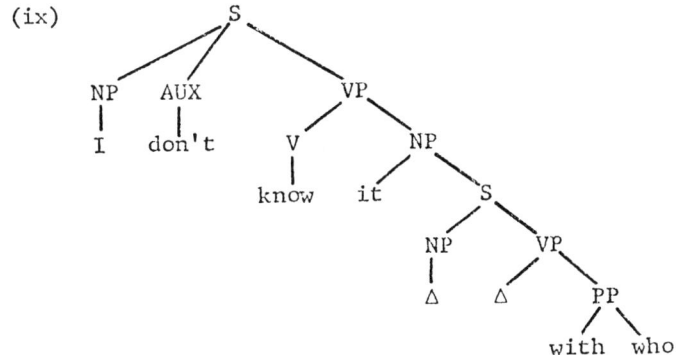

there is nothing to prevent the PP from preposing, to

produce sentence (viiib). Some ad-hoc principle would

have to be added to the effect that when in the <u>previous</u>

clause there is an idiomatic expression of a certain kind,

then the PP in the following clause could not be preposed.

The point of these examples is to show that (a)

Ross's arguments hold only for one possible interpretive

theory, but for another possible interpretive theory many

of his arguments fail, and (b) if one proposes an inter-

pretive theory of the sort sketched here one must show

how the problems mentioned can be overcome in some natural

fashion.

The basic idea behind an interpretive theory which

would posit unspecified nodes would be to reconstruct the

reading of the embedded question on the basis of the

reading of the previous clause. However, it is difficult to see how this could be truly different from a treatment which utilized deletion rules. The position we will take in this chapter, for reasons we discuss shortly, is that the existence of deletion rules such as Sluicing and VP-Deletion is not inconsistent with an interpretive treatment of anaphoric expressions. Thus, there is no need to press for an interpretive approach of the sort sketched in this note.

4. It is interesting to note that the notion of sloppy identity renders superfluous the suggestion by Lakoff [1967] that adverbial clauses originate from 'higher' sentences. Thus, for sentences such as:

> (i)   Goldwater won in the West, but it couldn't happen here.

Lakoff argues that the underlying structure must be roughly as follows:

(ii)

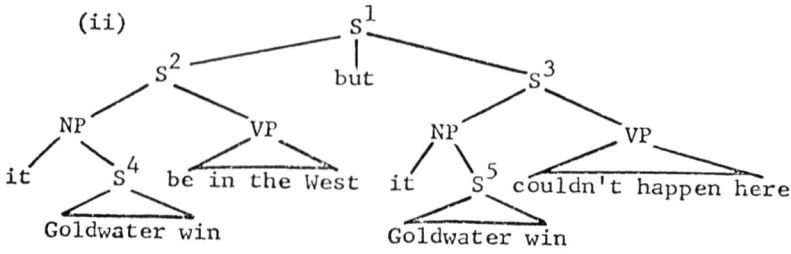

The structure in (ii) is motivated by the fact that the anaphoric expression _it_ in the second clause of (i) does not include in its interpretation the phrase in the West. If this phrase originates in a higher clause, the deep structure can be formulated such that S-Deletion can apply to delete S^5, with the proper interpretation. Thus, Lakoff argues that adverbial clauses in general originate in higher clauses.

Given sloppy identity, however, there is no evidence that adverbial clauses originate in a higher sentence, since S^2 in (ii) can be represented:

(iii)

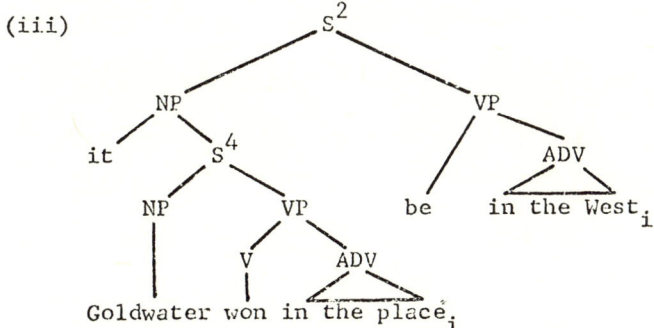

(S^3 would be represented in an analogous fashion). Adverbial clauses can still be generated in the sentences in which they appear in surface structure, and S-Deletion will overlook the differences in commanded pro-forms when deleting S^5. Hence, sloppy identity removes the motivation for positing adverbial clauses in higher sentences

5. Notice, incidentally, that the notion of sloppy identity
    presupposes a specific set of assumptions concerning pro-
    nominalization, in particular, assumptions concerning the
    level at which coreferentiality relationships are estab-
    lished. Since sloppy identity makes crucial use of the
    relation antecedent, this notion (or any other which makes
    use of the notion 'pronoun commanded by its antecedent')
    therefore presupposes that at the level at which various
    deletion rules apply, coreferentiality relationships have
    been established. For example, in a structure such as
    (53), it is crucial that at the time the deletion rule
    applies, referential indices have already been assigned
    (or any equivalent mechanism) since it must be determined
    whether the embedded pronouns are in fact commanded by
    their antecedents.

        If one accepts the arguments given by Lakoff [1968]
    that coreferentiality relationships which are assigned at
    a pre-surface level can be filtered by output conditions
    (hence, that potentially well-formed coreferentiality re-
    lationships can be ruled out at the surface level), then
    sloppy identity is in principle impossible. If one wishes
    to maintain sloppy identity, it must be shown that core-
    ference is determined prior to the application of deletion
    rules.

6. Note, however, that the interpretive principles must be
   further modified. That is, consider the possible interpretations for the following:

    (i)   John said that Bill complained that Mary threw
           garbage on the lawn, but you don't have to
           mention it.

The interpretation of the second clause of (i) is as
follows:

    (ii) a. You don't have to mention that John said
            that Bill complained that Mary threw garbage
            on the lawn.
         b. You don't have to mention that Bill complain-
            ed that Mary threw garbage on the lawn.
         c. You don't have to mention that Mary threw
            garbage on the lawn.

Hence, the anaphoric expression can refer to the most
deeply embedded clause, or to the next clause 'up', or
finally to the entire antecedent.

BIBLIOGRAPHY

Akmajian, Adrian [1970] "On Deriving Cleft Sentences from Pseudo-Cleft Sentences," Linguistic Inquiry 1:149-168.

Akmajian, Adrian and Ray S. Jackendoff [1970] "Coreferentiality and Stress," Linguistic Inquiry 1:124-126.

Anderson, Stephen R. [forthcoming,a] "How to Get Even," Linguistic Inquiry.

Anderson, Stephen R. [forthcoming,b] "A Little Light on the Role of Deep Structure in Semantic Interpretation," Foundations of Language.

Austin, J. [1962] How to Do Things With Words, Clarendon Press, Oxford, England.

Bach, Emmon [1967] "Have and Be in English Syntax," Language 43:462-485.

Bach, Emmon and Robert Harms, eds., [1968] Universals in Linguistic Theory, Holt, Rinehart, and Winston, New York.

Bach, Emmon and Stanley Peters [1968] "Pseudo-Cleft Sentences," Mimeographed.

Baker, C.L. [1968] Indirect Questions in English, University of Illinois Doctoral Dissertation.

Baker, C.L. [1970] "Notes on the Description of English Questions: The Role of an Abstract Question Morpheme," Foundations of Language 6:197-219.

Bolinger, D.L. [1965] Forms of English: Accent, Morpheme, Order, edited by Isamu Abe and Tetsuya Kanekiyo, Harvard University Press, Cambridge, Mass.

Bresnan, Joan [1970] "An Argument Against Pronominalization," Linguistic Inquiry 1:122-123.

Bresnan, Joan [1970] "On Complementizers: Toward a Syntactic Theory of Complement Types," in Mathematical Linguistics and Automatic Translation, Report No. NSF 24, Computation Laboratory, Harvard University.

Brook, G.L. [1964] A History of the English Language, W.W. Norton and Company, New York, New York.

Chomsky, Noam [1965] Aspects of the Theory of Syntax, M.I.T. Press, Cambridge, Mass.

Chomsky, Noam [1967] "Remarks on Nominalization," in Jacobs, R. and P.S. Rosenbaum, eds. [forthcoming].

Chomsky, Noam [1969] "Deep Structure, Surface Structure, and Semantic Interpretation," in Jakobovits and Steinberg, eds., [forthcoming].

Chomsky, Noam [1970] "Some Empirical Issues in the Theory of Transformational Grammar," Mimeographed, M.I.T.

Clifton, Ernest [1969] "The English Pseudo-Cleft," Unpublished Paper, M.I.T.

Culicover, Peter [1970] Syntactic and Semantic Investigations, M.I.T. Doctoral Dissertation.

Emonds, J.E. [1970] Root and Structure Preserving Transformations, M.I.T. Doctoral Dissertation.

Faraci, Bob [1970] "On the Deep Question of Pseudo-Clefts," Mimeographed, M.I.T.

Fischer, Susan D. [1968] "On Cleft Sentences and Contrastive Stress," Unpublished Paper, M.I.T.

Fraser, Bruce [1969] "An Analysis of Even in English," in Language Research Reports 1:II (1-34), Language Research Foundation, Cambridge, Mass.

Halliday, M.A.K. [1967] "Notes on Transitivity and Theme in English, Part 2," Journal of Linguistics 3:199-244.

Jackendoff, Ray [1966] "A Note on Selectional Restrictions," Unpublished Paper, M.I.T.

Jackendoff, Ray S. [1969] Some Rules of Semantic Interpretation for English, M.I.T. Doctoral Dissertation.

Jakobovits, L.A. and P.D. Steinberg, eds., [forthcoming] Semantics: An Interdisciplinary Reader in Philosophy, Psychology, Linguistics and Anthropology, The University of Illinois Press, Urbana, Illinois.

Jacobs, R. and P.S. Rosenbaum, eds. [forthcoming] Readings in English Transformational Grammar, Blaisdell-Ginn, Waltham, Mass.

Jakobson, Roman and S. Kawamoto, eds., Studies in General and Oriental Linguistics, Commemorative Volume for Dr. Shiro Hattori, TEC Corporation for Language Research, Tokyo.

Katz, J.J. and Paul M. Postal [1964] An Integrated Theory of Linguistic Descriptions, M.I.T. Press, Cambridge, Mass.

Kuno, Susumu [1969] "Some Properties of Non-Referential Noun Phrases," in Jakobson and Kawamoto, eds., [1970].

Lakoff, George [1965] On the Nature of Syntactic Irregularity, Mathematical Linguistics and Automatic Translation. Report No. NSF 16, Computation Laboratory, Harvard University.

Lakoff, George [1967] "Pronominalization, Negation, and the Analysis of Adverbs," Mimeographed, Harvard University.

Lakoff, George [1968] "Pronouns and Reference," Mimeographed, Harvard University.

Lakoff, George [1969] "On Generative Semantics," to appear in Jakobovits and Steinberg, eds., [forthcoming].

Lakoff, George [1970] "Presuppositions and Relative Grammaticality," in Mathematical Linguistics and Automatic Translation. Report No. NSF 24, Computation Laboratory, Harvard University.

Lasnik, Howard [1970] "The Scope of Negation," Mimeographed, M.I.T.

McCawley, James D. [1968] "The Role of Semantics in a Grammar," in Bach and Harms, eds., [1968].

Postal, Paul M. [1968] *Cross-Over Phenomena: A Study in the Grammar of Coreference*, I.B.M. Corporation, Thomas J. Watson Research Center, Yorktown Heights, New York.

Ross, J.R. [1967] *Constraints on Variables in Syntax*, M.I.T. Doctoral Dissertation.

Ross, J.R. [1968] "On Declarative Sentences," in Jacobs, R. and P.S. Rosenbaum [forthcoming].

Ross, J.R. [1969] "Guess Who?," in *Papers from the Fifth Regional Meeting of the Chicago Linguistic Society*, University of Chicago Linguistics Department, Chicago, Illinois.

Strawson, P.F. [1956] "On Referring," in *Essays in Conceptual Analysis*, A. Flew, ed., The Macmillan Company, New York.